Top 100 Motivational Stories

The Best Inspirational Short Stories And Anecdotes Of All Time

MEIR LIRAZ

Published by BizMove
www.bizmove.com

"God, grant me the serenity to accept the things I cannot change, the courage to change the things I can, and the wisdom to know the difference."
(Reinhold Niebuhr)

Introduction

For this book we scanned hundreds of motivational stories and anecdotes to bring you this collection of the top 100 inspirational short stories.

The stories here will open your eyes and give you valuable insights regarding success, love, money, achievement, overcoming obstacles, relationships, hope, positive thinking, life, happiness, family, leadership, dreams, appreciation, spiritual, uplifting, adversity, moving on, perseverance, inspiring words, people, encouraging, thoughts, faith, sports, inspiring sayings, friendship quotes, famous people, motivation and children.

Some of the stories will make you cry others will make you smile, none will leave you indifferent. You'll find them witty, touching, amusing, and spirit-soothing.

We hope you'll enjoy reading them as much as we enjoyed putting them together.

Are you ready to get empowered?

Weakness or Strength?

Sometimes your biggest weakness can become your biggest strength. Take, for example, the story of one 10-year-old boy who decided to study judo despite the fact that he had lost his left arm in a devastating car accident.

The boy began lessons with an old Japanese judo master. The boy was doing well, so he couldn't understand why, after three months of training the master had taught him only one move.

"Sensei," the boy finally said, "Shouldn't I be learning more moves?"

"This is the only move you know, but this is the only move you'll ever need to know," the sensei replied.

Not quite understanding, but believing in his teacher, the boy kept training.

Several months later, the sensei took the boy to his first tournament. Surprising himself, the boy easily won his first two matches. The third match proved to be more difficult, but after some time, his opponent became impatient and charged; the boy deftly used his one move to win the match. Still amazed by his success, the boy was now in the finals.

This time, his opponent was bigger, stronger, and more experienced. For a while, the boy appeared to be overmatched. Concerned that the boy might get hurt, the referee called a time-out. He was about to stop the match when the sensei intervened.

"No," the sensei insisted, "Let him continue."

Soon after the match resumed, his opponent made a critical mistake: he dropped his guard. Instantly, the boy used his move to pin him. The boy had won the match and the tournament. He was the champion.

On the way home, the boy and sensei reviewed every move in each and every match. Then the boy summoned the courage to ask what was really on his mind.

"Sensei, how did I win the tournament with only one move?"

"You won for two reasons," the sensei answered. "First, you've almost mastered one of the most difficult throws in all of judo. And second, the only known defense for that move is for your opponent to grip your left arm."

The boy's biggest weakness had become his biggest strength.

Your Personal Angel

A story about an angel who has been taking care of you even before you were born and will always take care no matter how much you grow old.... you know that angel as Mother, Mamma, Mom...

My mom only had one eye. I hated her... She was such an embarrassment. She cooked for students and teachers to support the family.

There was this one day during elementary school where my mom came to say hello to me. I was so embarrassed.

How could she do this to me? I ignored her, threw her a hateful look and ran out. The next day at school one of my classmates said, 'Eeee, your mom only has one eye!'

I wanted to bury myself. I also wanted my mom to just disappear. I confronted her that day and said, ' If you're only gonna make me a laughing stock, why don't you just die?'

My mom did not respond… I didn't even stop to think for a second about what I had said, because I was full of anger. I was oblivious to her feelings.

I wanted out of that house, and have nothing to do with her. So I studied real hard, got a chance to go abroad to study.

Then, I got married. I bought a house of my own. I had kids of my own. I was happy with my life, my kids and the comforts. Then one day, my Mother came to visit me. She hadn't seen me in years and she didn't even meet her grandchildren.

When she stood by the door, my children laughed at her, and I yelled at her for coming over uninvited. I screamed at her, 'How dare you come to my house and scare my children!' Get Out Of Here! Now!'

And to this, my mother quietly answered, 'Oh, I'm so sorry. I may have gotten the wrong address,' and she disappeared out of sight.

One day, a letter regarding a school reunion came to my house. So I lied to my wife that I was going on a business trip. After the reunion, I went to the old shack just out of curiosity.

My neighbors said that she died. I did not shed a single

tear. They handed me a letter that she had wanted me to have.

My dearest son,

I think of you all the time. I'm sorry that I came to your house and scared your children.

I was so glad when I heard you were coming for the reunion. But I may not be able to even get out of bed to see you. I'm sorry that I was a constant embarrassment to you when you were growing up.

You see... when you were very little, you got into an accident, and lost your eye. As a mother, I couldn't stand watching you having to grow up with one eye. So I gave you mine.

I was so proud of my son who was seeing a whole new world for me, in my place, with that eye.

With all my love to you,

Your mother

The Master's Hand

Wishing to encourage her young son's progress on the piano, a mother took the small boy to a concert of the famous pianist, Paderewski. After they were seated, the mother spotted a friend in the audience and walked down the aisle to greet her. Seizing the opportunity to explore the wonders of the concert hall, the little boy rose and eventually explored his way through a door marked "No Admittance."

When the house lights dimmed and the concert was about to begin, the mother returned to her seat and discovered that her son was missing. Suddenly, the curtains parted and the spotlights focused on the impressive Steinway piano on stage.

In horror, the mother saw her little boy sitting at the keyboard. Innocently, he then began to play "Chopsticks". The crowd reacted with anger, some shouts were heard, "Take the boy away!", "Who is bringing a little boy to a concert?!".

When Paderewski heard the uproar backstage, he grabbed his coat and rushed to the stage. Realizing what was going on, he went to the piano, Reaching around the little boy from behind, the master began to improvise a countermelody to "chopsticks." As the two of them played together, Paderewski kept whispering in the boy's ear, "Keep going. Don't quit, son... don't stop... don't stop."

Together, the old master and the little boy transformed an embarrassing situation into a wonderfully creative experience. The audience was mesmerized.

God Make Me A TV

Students at an elementary school were asked to write an essay about what they would like God to do for them. At the end of the day, while grading the essays, a teacher read one that made her very emotional.

Her husband, who had just walked in, saw her crying and asked her "What happened?" She answered "Read this. It is one of my school's students' essays.":

"Oh God, tonight I ask you something very special. Make me into a television set. I want to take its place and live like the TV in my house.

Have my own special place, and have my family around me. To be taken seriously when I talk. I want to be the center of attention and be heard without interruptions or questions.

I want to receive the same special care as the TV set receives even when it is not working. Have the company of my dad when he arrives home from work, even when he is tired. And I want my mom to want me when she is sad and upset, instead of ignoring me. And I want my brothers to fight to be with me.

I want to feel that family just leaves everything aside, every now and then, just to spend some time with me. And last but not least, ensure that I can make them all happy and entertain them. Lord I don't ask you for much. I just want to live like a TV."

At that moment the husband said "My God, poor kid. What horrible parents!"

The wife looked up at him and said "That essay is our son's!"

The Cookie Thief

A woman was waiting at an airport one night, with several long hours before her flight. She hunted for a book in the airport shops, bought a bag of cookies and found a place to drop.

She was engrossed in her book but happened to see, that the man sitting beside her, as bold as could be... grabbed a cookie or two from the bag in between, which she tried to ignore to avoid a scene.

So she munched the cookies and watched the clock, as the gutsy cookie thief diminished her stock. She was getting more irritated as the minutes ticked by, thinking, "If I wasn't so nice, I would blacken his eye."

With each cookie she took, he took one too, when only one was left, she wondered what he would do. With a smile on his face, and a nervous laugh, he took the last cookie and broke it in half.

He offered her half, as he ate the other, she snatched it from him and thought... Oooh, brother. This guy has some nerve and he's also rude, why he didn't even show any gratitude!

She had never known when she had been so galled, and sighed with relief when her flight was called. She gathered her belongings and headed to the gate, refusing to look back at the thieving ingrate.

She boarded the plane, and sank in her seat, then she sought her book, which was almost complete. As she reached in her baggage, she gasped with surprise, there was her bag of cookies, in front of her eyes.

If mine are here, she moaned in despair, the others were his, and he tried to share. Too late to apologize, she realized with grief, that she was the rude one, the ingrate, the thief.

The Whole World Stinks

Wise men and philosophers throughout the ages have disagreed on many things, but many are in unanimous agreement on one point: "We become what we think about." Ralph Waldo Emerson said, "A man is what he thinks about all day long." The Roman emperor Marcus Aurelius put it this way: "A man's life is what his thoughts make of it." In the Bible we find: "As a man thinks in his heart, so is he."

One Sunday afternoon, a cranky grandfather was visiting his family. As he lay down to take a nap, his grandson decided to have a little fun by putting Limburger cheese on Grandfather's mustache. Soon, grandpa awoke with a snort and charged out of the bedroom saying, "This room stinks." Through the house he went, finding every room smelling the same. Desperately he made his way outside only to find that "The whole world stinks!"

So it is when we fill our minds with negativism. Everything we experience and everybody we encounter will carry the scent we hold in our mind.

The Baker and the Farmer

A baker in a little country town bought the butter he used from a nearby farmer. One day he suspected that the bricks of butter were not full pounds, and for several days he weighed them.

He was right. They were short weight, and he had the farmer arrested.

At the trial the judge said to the farmer, "I presume you have scales?"

"No, your honor."

"Then how do you manage to weigh the butter you sell?" inquired the judge.

The farmer replied, "That's easily explained, your honor. I have balances and for a weight I use a one-pound loaf I buy from the baker."

Moral of the story: In life, you get what you give. Don't try and cheat others.

Complain! Complain! Complain!

It takes a disciplined spirit to endure the monastery on

Mount Serat in Spain. One of the fundamental requirements of this religious order is that the young men must maintain silence. Opportunities to speak are scheduled once every two years, at which time they are allowed to speak only two words.

One young initiate in this religious order, who had completed his first two years of training, was invited by his superior to make his first two-word presentation. "Food terrible," he said.

Two years later the invitation was once again extended. The young man used this forum to exclaim, "Bed lumpy."

Arriving at his superior's office two years later he proclaimed, "I quit." The superior looked at this young monk and said, "You know, it doesn't surprise me a bit. All you've done since you arrived is complain, complain, complain.

Exaggerated? Maybe. What if you were asked to share two words that describe your Life? Would your focus be the lumps, bumps, and unfairness, or are you committed to dwell on those things that are good, right, and lovely?

The Mountain

There were two warring tribes in the Andes, one that lived in the lowlands and the other high in the mountains. The mountain people invaded the lowlanders one day, and as part of their plundering of the people, they kidnapped a baby of one of the lowlander families and took the infant with them back up into the mountains.

The lowlanders didn't know how to climb the mountain. They didn't know any of the trails that the mountain people used, and they didn't know where to find the mountain people or how to track them in the steep terrain.

Even so, they sent out their best party of fighting men to climb the mountain and bring the baby home.

The men tried first one method of climbing and then another. They tried one trail and then another. After several days of effort, however, they had climbed only several hundred feet.

Feeling hopeless and helpless, the lowlander men decided that the cause was lost, and they prepared to return to their village below.

As they were packing their gear for the descent, they saw the baby's mother walking toward them. They realized that she was coming down the mountain that they hadn't figured out how to climb.

And then they saw that she had the baby strapped to her back. How could that be?

One man greeted her and said, "We couldn't climb this mountain. How did you do this when we, the strongest and most able men in the village, couldn't do it?"

She shrugged her shoulders and said, "It wasn't your baby."

Blurred Vision

A businessman was highly critical of his competitors' storefront windows. "Why, they are the dirtiest windows in town," he claimed. Fellow business people grew tired of the man's continual criticism and nitpicking comments about the windows. One day over coffee, the businessman carried the subject just too far.

Before leaving, a fellow store owner suggested the man get his own windows washed. He followed the advice, and the next day at coffee, he exclaimed, "I can't believe it. As soon as I washed my windows, my competitor must have cleaned his too. You should see them shine."

Confucius once declared, "Don't complain about the snow on your neighbor's roof when your own doorstep is unclean."

Two Apples

A lovely little girl was holding two apples with both hands. Her mom came in and softly asked her little daughter with a smile: my sweetie, could you give your mom one of your two apples?

The girl looked up at her mom for some seconds, then she suddenly took a quick bite on one apple, and then quickly on the other. The mom felt the smile on her face freeze.

She tried hard not to reveal her disappointment.

Then the little girl handed one of her bitten apples to her mom, and said: mommy, here you are. This is the sweeter one.

No matter who you are, how experienced you are, and how knowledgeable you think you are, always delay judgment. Give others the privilege to explain themselves. What you see may not be the reality. Never conclude for others.

Paradise and Hell

A soldier named Nobushige came to Hakuin, the famous Zen master, and asked: "Is there really a paradise and a hell?"

"Who are you?" inquired Hakuin.

"I am a samurai," the warrior replied.

"You, a soldier!" exclaimed Hakuin. "What kind of ruler would have you as his guard? Your face looks like that of a beggar."

Nobushige became so angry that he began to draw his sword, but Hakuin continued: "So you have a sword! Your weapon is probably much too dull to cut off my head."

As Nobushige drew his sword Hakuin remarked: "Here open the gates of hell!"

At these words the samurai, perceiving the master's

discipline, sheathed his sword and bowed.

"Here open the gates of paradise," said Hakuin.

The Touch

It was battered and scarred, and the auctioneer thought it scarcely worth his while to waste much time on the old violin. But he held it up with a smile:

"What am I biddin' good folks," He cried. "Who'll start the biddin' for me? A dollar;" then, "Two! Only two? Two dollars, and who'll make it three? Three dollars once, three dollars twice; going for three --- " But no.

From the room, far back, a gray-haired man came forward and picked up the bow. Then, wiping the dust from the old violin, and tightening the loose strings, he played a melody pure and sweet as a carolling angel's wings.

There's many a man with life out of tune, who's battered and scarred, and is auctioned cheap to the thoughtless crowd, much like the old violin. A mess of potage, a glass of wine, a game, and he travels on. He is going once, and going twice, he's going and almost gone.

But the Master comes, and the foolish crowd never can quite understand the worth of a soul, and the change that's wrought by the touch of the Master's Hand.

Cleaning Up Our Mistakes

Pencil: I'm sorry.

Eraser: For what? You didn't do anything wrong.

Pencil: I'm sorry, you get hurt because of me. Whenever I made a mistake, you're always there to erase it. But as you make my mistakes vanish, you lose a part of yourself and get smaller and smaller each time.

Eraser: That's true, but I don't really mind. You see, I was made to do this, I was made to help you whenever you do something wrong, even though one day I know I'll be gone. I'm actually happy with my job. So please, stop worrying I hate seeing you sad.

Our Parents are like the eraser, whereas we children are the pencil. They're always there for their children, cleaning up their mistakes. Sometimes along the way they get hurt and become smaller (older and eventually pass on) Take care of your Parents, treat them with kindness and most especially love them.

A Glass Of Milk

A young poor boy who was begging from door to door to feed his hungry stomach, decided he would ask for a meal at the next house. However, he lost his nerve when a lovely young woman opened the door. Instead of a meal, he just asked for a glass of water, the woman thought he looked hungry, so she brought him a large glass of milk. He drank it slowly, and then asked "how much do I owe you?."

"You don't owe me anything, she replied. Mother has taught us never to accept pay for kindness." He said, "Then I thank you from my heart".

Years later, that young woman became critically ill, the local doctors were battling because they couldn't cure her, they finally sent her to the big city, where they called specialists to study her rare illness.

Dr. Howard Kelly was called in for the consultation, when he heard the name of the town where she came from, a strange light filled his eyes. Immediately, he rose and went down the hall of the hospital to her room. He recognized her at once.

He went back to the consultation room determined to do his best to save her life. From that day, he gave special attention to that case. After a long struggle, the battle was won! Dr. Kelly requested the business office to pass the final bill to him for approval. He looked at it, then wrote something on the bill. It was sent to her room, the woman feared opening it, for she was sure it might take the rest of her life to pay for it all.

Finally she looked, and noticed something was written at the edge of the note, 'paid in full with a glass of milk'. Tears filled her eyes as she immediately remembered...

Every form of kindness you show doesn't bounce, it reproduces itself. Not necessarily before your eyes, but it always does. It is good to be good. Always be nice for it always comes back to you.

Post-it Notes

The 3M Company used to encourages creativity from its employees. The company allowed its researchers to spend 15 percent of their time on any project that interests them. This attitude has brought fantastic benefits not only to the employees but to the 3M Company itself. Many times, a spark of an idea turned into a successful product that has boosted 3M's profits tremendously.

Some years ago, a scientist in 3M's commercial office took advantage of this 15 percent creative time. This scientist, Art Fry, came up with an idea for one of 3M's best-selling products. It seems that Art Fry dealt with a small irritation every Sunday as he sang in the church choir. After marking his pages in the hymnal with small bits of paper, the small pieces would invariably fall out all over the floor.

Suddenly, an idea struck Fry. He remembered an adhesive developed by a colleague that everyone thought was a failure because it did not stick very well. "I coated the adhesive on a paper sample," Fry recalls, "and I found that it was not only a good bookmark, but it was great for writing notes. It will stay in place as long as you want it to, and then you can remove it without damage."

Yes, Art Fry hit the jackpot. The resulting product was called Post-it! and has become one of 3M's most successful office products.

"I Can Make It Happen"

History abounds with tales of experts who were convinced that the ideas, plans, and projects of others could never be achieved. However, accomplishment came to those who said, "I can make it happen."

The Italian sculptor Agostino d'Antonio worked diligently on a large piece of marble. Unable to produce his desired masterpiece, he lamented, "I can do nothing with it." Other sculptors also worked this difficult piece of marble, but to no avail. Michelangelo discovered the stone and visualized the possibilities in it. His "I-can-make-it-happen" attitude resulted in one of the world's masterpieces - David.

The experts of Spain concluded that Columbus's plans to discover a new and shorter route to India was virtually impossible. Queen Isabella and King Ferdinand ignored the report of the experts. "I can make it happen," Columbus persisted. And he did. Most people at that time "knew" the world was flat, but not Columbus. The Nina, the Pinta, the Santa Maria, along with Columbus and his small band of followers, sailed to "impossible" new lands and thriving resources.

Even the great Thomas Alva Edison discouraged his friend, Henry Ford, from pursuing his fledgling idea of a motorcar. Convinced of the worthlessness of the idea, Edison invited Ford to come and work for him. Ford remained committed and tirelessly pursued his dream. Although his first attempt resulted in a vehicle without reverse gear, Henry Ford knew he could make it happen.

And, of course, he did.

Let's not forget our friends Orville and Wilbur Wright. Journalists, friends, armed forces specialists, and even their father laughed at the idea of an airplane. "What a silly and insane way to spend money. Leave flying to the birds," they jeered. "Sorry," the Wright brothers responded. "We have a dream, and we can make it happen." As a result, a place called Kitty Hawk, North Carolina, became the setting for the launching of their "ridiculous" idea.

Finally, as you read these accounts under the magnificent lighting of your environment, consider the plight of Benjamin Franklin. He was admonished to stop the foolish experimenting with lighting. What an absurdity and waste of time! Why, nothing could outdo the fabulous oil lamp. Thank goodness Franklin knew he could make it happen.

You too can make it happen!

The Apple Tree

A long time ago, there was a huge apple tree. A little boy loved to come and play around it every day. He climbed to the treetop, ate the apples, and took a nap under it. He loved the tree and the tree loved to play with him. Time went by, the little boy had grown up and he no longer played around the tree every day. One day, the boy came back to the tree and he looked sad. "Come and play with me", the tree asked the boy. "I am no longer a kid, I do not play around trees anymore," the boy replied. "I want toys. I need money to buy them."

"Sorry, but I do not have money, but you can pick all my apples and sell them. So, you will have money." The boy was so excited. He grabbed all the apples on the tree and left happily. The boy never came back after he picked the apples. The tree was sad.

One day, the boy who now turned into a man returned and the tree was excited. "Come and play with me" the tree said. "I do not have time to play. I have to work for my family. We need a house for shelter. Can you help me?"

"Sorry, but I do not have any house. But you can chop off my branches to build your house." So the man cut all the branches of the tree and left happily. The tree was glad to see him happy but the man never came back since then. The tree was again lonely and sad.

One hot summer day, the man returned and the tree was delighted. "Come and play with me!" The tree said.

"I am getting old. I want to go sailing to relax myself. Can you give me a boat?" Said the man.

"Use my trunk to build your boat. You can sail far away and be happy." So the man cut the tree trunk to make a boat. He went sailing and never showed up for a long time.

Finally, the man returned after many years. "Sorry, my boy. But I do not have anything for you anymore. No more apples for you", the tree said. "No problem, I do not have any teeth to bite" the man replied.

"No more trunk for you to climb on." "I am too old for that now" the man said.

"I really cannot give you anything, the only thing left is my dying roots," the tree said with tears.

"I do not need much now, just a place to rest. I am tired after all these years," the man replied. "Good! Old tree roots are the best place to lean on and rest, come sit down with me and rest." The man sat down and the tree was glad and smiled with tears.

This is a story of everyone. The tree is like our parents. When we were young, we loved to play with our Mom and Dad. When we grow up, we leave them; only come to them when we need something or when we are in trouble. No matter what, parents will always be there and give everything they could just to make you happy.

A Tribute To Mother

He was a young boy who lived with his elderly mother. His mother wanted him to learn how to play the piano because she longed to hear her son play for her.

She sent her son to a piano teacher who took Robby in under her guidance. However, there was one small problem because Robby was not musically inclined and therefore was very slow in learning.

The teacher did not have much faith in the boy because of his weakness. However, The mother was very enthusiastic and every week she would send Robby to the teacher.

One day Robby stopped attending the piano lessons. The

teacher thought that he had given up and in fact she was quite pleased since she did not give much hope to Robby.

Not long after, the piano teacher was given the task to organize a piano concert in town. She sent out circulars to invite the students and public to attend the event. Suddenly, she received a call from Robby who offered to take part in the concert. The teacher told Robby that he was not good enough and that he was no longer a student since he had stopped coming for lessons.

Robby begged her to give him a chance and promised that he would not let her down. Finally, she gave in but scheduled him to play last, hoping that he will change his mind at the last minute.

When the big day came, the hall was packed and the children gave their best performance. Finally, it was Robby's turn to play and as his name was announced, he walked in. He was not in proper attire and his hair was not properly groomed. The teacher was really nervous since Robby's performance could spoil the whole evening's brilliant performance.

As Robby started playing the crowd became silent and was amazed at the skill of this little boy. In fact, he gave the best performance of the evening. At the end of his presentation the crowd and the piano teacher gave him a standing ovation.

The crowd asked Robby how he managed to play so brilliantly. With a microphone in front of him, he said, "I was not able to attend the weekly piano lessons as there was no one to send me because my mother was sick with cancer. She just passed away and I wanted her to hear me play. You see, this is the first time she is able to hear me play because when she was alive she was deaf and now I know she is listening to me. I have to play my best for her!"

When you have a passion and a reason to do something, you will surely excel. You may not be talented or gifted but if you have a strong enough reason to do something, you will be able to tap into your inner given potential. "When there is a will, there is a way".

Things We Can Learn from a Dog...

Never pass up the opportunity to go for a joy ride.

Allow the experience of fresh air and the wind in your face to be pure ecstasy.

When loved ones come home, always run to greet them.

When it's in your best interest, practice obedience.

Let others know when they've invaded your territory.

Take naps and stretch before rising.

Run, romp and play daily.

Eat with gusto and enthusiasm.

Be loyal.

Never pretend to be something you're not.

If what you want lies buried, dig until you find it.

When someone is having a bad day, be silent, sit close by and nuzzle them gently.

Thrive on attention and let people touch you.

Avoid biting when a simple growl will do.

On hot days, drink lots of water and lie under a shady tree.

When you're happy, dance around and wag your entire body.

No matter how often you're scolded, don't buy into the guilt thing and pout .. run right back and make friends.

Delight in the simple joys of a long walk.

Acres Of Diamonds

There was a farmer in Africa who was happy and content. He was happy because he was content. He was content because he was happy. One day a business man came to him and told him about the glory of diamonds and the power that goes along with them.

The man said, "If you had a diamond the size of your thumb, you could have your own city. If you had a diamond the size of your fist, you could probably own your own country." And then he went away.

That night the farmer couldn't sleep. He was unhappy and

he was discontent. He was unhappy because he was discontent and discontent because he was unhappy. The next morning he made arrangements to sell off his farm, took care of his family and went in search of diamonds.

.

He looked all over Africa and couldn't find any. For several years he walked from country to country, from river to river, until at some point he was emotionally, physically and financially broke. He got so disheartened that he threw himself into a river and died.

.

Back home, the person who had bought his farm was watering the sheep at a stream that ran through the farm. Across the stream, the rays of the morning sun hit a stone and made it sparkle like a rainbow. He thought it would look good on his living room's chest. He picked up the stone and put it in the living room.

That afternoon the business man came and saw the stone sparkling. He asked, "Is Hafiz back?" The new owner said, "No, why do you ask?" The business man said, "Because that is a diamond. I recognize one when I see one."

The man said, "No, that's just a stone I picked up from the stream. Come, I'll show you. There are many more." They went and picked some samples and sent them for analysis. Sure enough, the stones were diamonds. They found that the farm was indeed covered with acres and acres of diamonds.

What is the moral of this story? Opportunity is always under our feet. We don't have to go anywhere. All we need to do is recognize it.

An Encounter At McDonalds

A touching story I received from a friend long ago and now sharing it with you. I don't have any idea about the original author.

I am a mother of three (ages 14, 12, 3) and have recently completed my college degree. The last class I had to take was Sociology. The teacher was absolutely inspiring with the qualities that I wish every human being had been graced with. Her last project of the term was called "Smile". The class was asked to go out and smile at three people and document their reaction.

I am a very friendly person and always smile at everyone and say hello anyway... so, I thought, this would be a piece of cake.

Soon after we were assigned the project, my husband, our youngest son, and I went out to a McDonalds. We were standing in line, waiting to be served, when all of a sudden everyone around us began to back away, and then even my husband did. I did not move an inch... an overwhelming feeling of panic welled up inside of me as I turned to see why they had moved.

As I turned around I smelled a horrible "dirty body" smell... and there standing behind me were two homeless men. As I looked down at the short gentleman, close to me, he was "smiling", his beautiful sky blue eyes were full of light as he searched for acceptance.

He said, "Good day" as he counted the few coins he had been clutching. The second man fumbled with his hands as he stood behind his friend. I realized the second man was mentally deficient and the blue eyed gentleman was his salvation. I held my tears as I stood there with them.

The young lady at the counter asked him what they wanted. He said, "Coffee is all Miss" because that was all they could afford (to sit in the restaurant and warm up they had to buy something... they just wanted to be warm).

Then I really felt it... the compulsion was so great I almost reached out and embraced the little man with the blue eyes. That is when I noticed all eyes in the restaurant were set on me... judging my every action. I smiled and asked the young lady behind the counter to give me two more breakfast meals on a separate tray. I then walked around the corner to the table that the men had chosen as a resting spot.

I put the tray on the table and laid my hand on the blue eyed gentleman's cold hand. He looked up at me, with tears in his eyes, and said, "Thank you". I leaned over, began to pat his hand, I couldn't say a word. I started to cry as I walked away to join my husband and son. When I sat down my husband smiled at me and said, "That is why God gave you to me honey....to give me hope". We held hands for a moment and looked at each other.

I returned to college, on the last evening of class, with this story in hand. I turned in "my project" and the instructor read it... then she looked up at me and said, "Can I share this?" I slowly nodded as she got the attention of the class. She began to read and that is when I knew that we as human beings share this need to heal.

In my own way I had touched the people at that McDonalds, my husband, son, instructor, and every soul that shared the classroom on the last night I spent as a college student. I Graduated with one of the biggest lessons I would ever learn... unconditional acceptance... after all... we are here to learn!

When God Made Fathers

When the good Lord was creating Fathers, he started with a tall frame.

A female angel nearby said, "What kind of a Father is that? If you're going to make children so close to the ground, why have you put the Father up so high? He won't be able to shoot marbles without kneeling, tuck a child in bed without bending, or even kiss a child without stooping"

God smiled and said, "Yes, but if I make him child size, who would children have to look up to?"

And when God made a Father's hands, they were large. The angel shook her head and said, "Large hands can't manage diaper pins, small buttons, rubber bands on pony tails, or even remove splinters caused from baseball bats."

Again God smiled and said, "I know, but they're large enough to hold everything a small boy empties from his pockets, yet small enough to cup a child's face in them."

Then God molded long slim legs and broad shoulders, "Do you realize you just made a Father without a lap?" The angel chuckled.

God said, "A Mother needs a lap. A Father needs strong shoulders to pull a sled, to balance a boy on a bicycle, or to hold a sleepy head on the way home from the circus."

When God was in the middle of creating the biggest feet any one had ever seen, the angel could not contain herself any longer. "That's not fair. Do you honestly think those feet are going to get out of bed early in the morning when the baby cries, or walk through a birthday party without crushing one or two of the guests?"

God again smiled and said, "They will work. You will see. They will support a small child who wants to ride to Banbury Cross or scare mice away from a summer cabin, or display shoes that will be a challenge to fill." God worked throughout the night, giving the Father few words, but a firm authoritative voice; eyes that see everything, but remain calm and tolerant.

Finally, almost as an after a thought, He added tears. Then he turned to the angel and said, "Now are you satisfied he can love as much as a Mother can?"

The angel said nothing more.

A World Of Green

Many years ago, in India, there was a rich man who was suffering from a severe eye pain. He consulted with numerous physicians and was getting multiple treatments.

He did not stop consulting a galaxy of medical experts; he consumed heavy loads of drugs and got hundreds of injections. But the pain persisted with greater vigor than before.

At last a monk who was supposed to be an expert in treating such patients was called for by the millionaire. The monk understood his problem and told him that for a certain period of time he should concentrate only on green colors and not look at any other color.

The rich man assembled a group of painters, purchased barrels of green color and directed that every object his eye was likely to fall on to be painted in green just as the monk had directed.

When the monk came to visit him after a few days, the rich man's servants ran with buckets of green paint and poured on him since he was wearing a red gown, lest their master not see any other color and his eye pain would come back.

Hearing this the monk laughed and said to the rich man "If only you had purchased a pair of green glasses, worth just a few Rupee, you could have saved these walls and trees and pots and all other articles and also could have saved a large share of your fortune. You cannot paint the whole world green."

Once we change our vision the world will appear accordingly. It is foolish to try to shape the world, let us shape ourselves first.

And in the same context (Attributed to an known monk):

"When I was a young man, I wanted to change the world.

I found it was difficult to change the world, so I tried to change my nation.

When I found I couldn't change the nation, I began to focus on my town.

I couldn't change the town and as an older man, I tried to change my family.

Now, as an old man, I realize the only thing I can change is myself,
and suddenly I realize that if long ago I had changed myself,
I could have made an impact on my family.

My family and I could have made an impact on our town.
Their impact could have changed the nation and
I could indeed have changed the world."

On Relationships

Woody Allen said it best when asked about "relationships," and he told a story to illustrate. He said I think this story speaks about relationships.

A man came in to see a psychiatrist. When the psychiatrist asked him what the problem was, the man said, "Well, it's my brother. I think he's crazy."

"Why do you think that," asked the Doctor.

"Well," said the man, "He thinks he's a chicken."

"Hmmm .." the doctor replied, "That does sound sort of strange. Why don't you bring him in."

"I can't," said the man.

"Well, why not," asked the doctor.

"Because, I need the eggs." the man said.

I guess we are intertwined a little more than we like to think. And, we always see the other's strangeness even though we have just as much of our own strangeness, and often we have "complimentary" strangeness.

The Perfect Girl

A friend asked a gentleman how it is that he never married?

Replied the gentleman, "Well, I guess I just never met the right woman... I guess I've been looking for the perfect girl."

"Oh, come on now," said the friend, "Surely you have met at least one girl that you wanted to marry."

"Yes, there was one girl .. once. I guess she was the one perfect girl... the only perfect girl I really ever met. She was just the right everything .. I really mean that she was the perfect girl for me."

"Well, why didn't you marry her," asked the friend.

"She was looking for the perfect man," he said.

Hang In There

Nicolo Paganini was a well-known and gifted nineteenth century violinist. He was also well known as a great showman with a quick sense of humor. His most memorable concert was in Italy with a full orchestra. He was performing before a packed house and his technique was incredible, his tone was fantastic, and his audience dearly loved him.

Toward the end of his concert, Paganini was astounding his audience with an unbelievable composition when suddenly one string on his violin snapped and hung limply from his instrument. Paganini frowned briefly, shook his head, and continued to play, improvising beautifully.

Then to everyone's surprise, a second string broke. And shortly thereafter, a third. Almost like a slapstick comedy, Paganini stood there with three strings dangling from his Stradivarius. But instead of leaving the stage, Paganini stood his ground and calmly completed the difficult number on the one remaining string.

Human Life Span

On the first day God created the dog. God said, "Sit all day by the door of your house and bark at anyone who comes in or walks past. I will give you a life span of twenty years." The dog said, "That's too long to be barking. Give me ten years and I'll give you back the other ten." So God agreed.

On the second day God created the monkey. God said, "Entertain people, do monkey tricks and make them laugh. I'll give you a twenty-year life span." The monkey said, "Monkey tricks for twenty years? I don't think so. Dog gave you back Ten, so that's what I'll do too, okay?" And God agreed.

On the third day God created the cow. "You must go to the field with the farmer all day long and suffer under the sun, have calves, and give milk to support the farmer. I will give you a life span of sixty years."

The cow said, "That's kind of a tough life you want me to live for sixty years. Let me have twenty and I'll give back the other forty." And God agreed again.

On the fourth day God created man. God said, "Eat, sleep, play, marry and enjoy your life. I'll give you twenty years."

Man said, "What? Only twenty years? Tell you what, I'll take my twenty, and the forty the cow gave back, and the ten the monkey gave back, and the ten the dog gave back, that makes eighty, okay?"

Okay," said God, "You've got a deal."

So that is why the first twenty years we eat, sleep, play, and enjoy ourselves; the next forty years we slave in the sun to support our family; the next ten years we do monkey tricks to entertain the grandchildren; and the last Ten years we sit on the front porch and bark at everyone.

Life has now been explained to you...

Two Horses

Just up the road from my home is a field, with two horses in it. From a distance, each horse looks like any other horse. But if you get a closer look you will notice something quite interesting...

One of the horses is blind.

His owner has chosen not to have him put down, but has made him a safe and comfortable barn to live in. This alone is pretty amazing.

But if you stand nearby and listen, you will hear the sound of a bell. It is coming from a smaller horse in the field. Attached to the horse's halter is a small, copper-colored bell. It lets the blind friend know where the other horse is, so he can follow.

As you stand and watch these two friends you'll see that the horse with the bell is always checking on the blind horse, and that the blind horse will listen for the bell and then slowly walk to where the other horse is, trusting he will not be led astray.

When the horse with the bell returns to the shelter of the barn each evening, he will stop occasionally to look back, making sure that the blind friend isn't too far behind to hear the bell.

Like the owners of these two horses, God does not throw us away just because we are not perfect. Or because we have problems or challenges. He watches over us and even brings others into our lives to help us when we are in need.

Sometimes we are the blind horse, being guided by the little ringing bell of those who were placed in our lives. And at other times we are the guide horse, helping others to find their way.

Lunch With God

A little boy wanted to meet God. He packed his backpack with two sets of clothes and some pieces of cake and he started his journey. He walked for a while until he felt tired.

So he sat in a park on the way, opened his backpack and took a piece of cake to eat. Then he noticed an old woman sitting sad nearby, so he offered her a piece of cake.

She gratefully accepted it with a wide look and smiled at him. Her smile was so pretty that the boy longed to see it again. After some time he offered her another piece of cake. Again, she accepted it and smiled at him.

The boy was delighted! They sat there all afternoon eating and smiling, but they never said a word.

While it grew dark, the boy was frightened and he got up to leave, but before he had gone more than a few steps, he ran back and gave her a hug and she in return kissed him with her prettiest smile.

When the boy returned home and opened the door, his mother was surprised by the look of joy on his face. She asked him, "What did you do today that made you look so happy?"

He replied," I had lunch with God."

Before his mother could respond, he added, "You know what? She's got the most beautiful smile I've ever seen in my life!"

Meanwhile, the old woman, also radiant with joy, returned to her home. Her son was stunned by the look of peace on her face and asked, "Mom, what did you do today that made you so happy?

She replied, "I ate cakes in the park with God." Before her son responded, she added, "You know, he's much younger than I expected."

Too often we underestimate the power of a touch, a smile, a kind word, a listening ear, an honest compliment or the smallest act of caring, all of which have the potential to turn a life around.

Remember, nobody knows how God looks like. People come into our lives for a reason, for a season, or for a lifetime. Accept all of them equally... And let them see God in you!

The Angry Father

A doctor entered the hospital in a hurry after being called in for an urgent surgery. He answered the call ASAP, changed his clothes and went directly to the surgery room.

He found the boy's father pacing in the hall waiting for the doctor. On seeing him, the dad yelled:

"Why did you take all this time to come? Don't you know that my son's life is in danger? Don't you have any sense of responsibility?"

The doctor smiled and said: "I am sorry, I wasn't in the hospital and I came as fast as I could after receiving the call... And now, I wish you'd calm down so that I can do my work"

"Calm down?! What if your son was in this room right now, would you calm down? If your own son dies now what will you do?" Said the father angrily.

The doctor smiled again and replied: doctors cannot prolong lives. Go and intercede for your son, we will do our best to help him"

"Giving advises when we're not concerned is so easy" Murmured the father.

The surgery took some hours after which the doctor went out content, "Thank goodness!, your son is saved!" And without waiting for the father's reply he carried on his way running. "If you have any question, ask the nurse!"

"Why is he so arrogant? He couldn't wait some minutes so that I could ask about my son's state" Commented the father when seeing the nurse minutes after the doctor left.

The nurse answered, tears coming down her face: "His son died yesterday in a road accident, he was attending the burial when we called him for your son's surgery. And now that he saved your son's life, he left running to finish his son's burial."

Moral: do not judge anyone... because you never know how their life is and what they're going through.

"Never criticize a man until you've walked a mile in his moccasins" (~American Indian Proverb)

Be A Lake

The old Master instructed an unhappy young man to put a handful of salt in a glass of water and then to drink it. "How does it taste?" the Master asked.

"Awful," spat the apprentice.

The Master chuckled and then asked the young man to take another handful of salt and put it in the lake.

The two walked in silence to the nearby lake and when the apprentice swirled his handful of salt into the lake, the old man said, "Now drink from the lake." As the water dripped down the young man's chin, the Master asked, "How does it taste?"Good!" remarked the apprentice.

"Do you taste the salt?" asked the Master. "No," said the young man. The Master sat beside this troubled young man, took his hands, and said, "The pain of life is pure salt; no more, no less. The amount of pain in life remains the same, exactly the same. But the amount we taste the 'pain' depends on the container we put it into. So when you are in pain, the only thing you can do is to enlarge your sense of things."

Stop being a Glass, Become a Lake!

Xvxry Pxrson Is Important

Years ago, before the personal computer, people where using typewriters. One manager let employees know how valuable they are with the following memo:

"You Arx A Kxy Pxrson"

Xvxn though my typxwritxr is an old modxl, it works vxry wxll -- xxcxpt for onx kxy. You would think that with all thx othxer kxys functioning propxrly, onx kxy not working would hardly bx noticxd; but just onx kxy out of whack sxxms to ruin thx wholx xffort.

You may say to yoursxlf -- Wxll, I'm only onx pxrson. No onx will noticx if I don't do my bxst. But it doxs makx a diffxrxncx, bxcausx an xffxctivx organization nxxds activx participation by xvxry onx to thx bxst of his or hxr ability.

So, thx nxxt timx you think you arx not important, rxmxmbxr my old typxwritxr. You arx a kxy pxrson.

Digging Up A Garden

An old man lived alone in Minnesota. He wanted to spade his potato garden, but it was very hard work. His only son, who would have helped him, was in prison. The old man wrote a letter to his son and mentioned his situation:

43

Dear Son,

I am feeling pretty bad because it looks like I won't be able to plant my potato garden this year. I hate to miss doing the garden because your mother always loved planting them. I'm just getting too old to be digging up a garden plot. If you were here, all my troubles would be over. I know you would dig the plot for me, if you weren't in prison.

Love,
Dad

Shortly, the old man received this telegram:

'For Heaven's sake, Dad, don't dig up the garden! That's where I buried the guns!'

At 4 a.m. the next morning, a dozen FBI agents and local police officers showed up and dug up the entire garden without finding any guns.

Confused, the old man wrote another note to his son telling him what had happened, and asked him what to do next.

His son's reply was:

'Go ahead and plant your potatoes, Dad. It's the best I could do for you from here.'

Moral of the story: No matter where you are in the world, if you have decided to do something deep from your heart, you can do it. It is the thought that matters, not where you are or where the person is.

The Secret of Growing Good Corn

There once was a farmer who grew award-winning corn. Each year he entered his corn in the state fair where it won a blue ribbon.

One year a newspaper reporter interviewed him and learned something interesting about how he grew it. The reporter discovered that the farmer shared his award winning corn seeds with his neighbors.

"How can you afford to share your best seed corn with your neighbors when they are entering corn in competition with yours each year?" the reporter asked.

"Why sir," said the farmer, "didn't you know? The wind picks up pollen from the ripening corn and swirls it from field to field. If my neighbors grow inferior corn, cross-pollination will steadily degrade the quality of my corn. If I am to grow good corn, I must help my neighbors grow good corn."

He is very much aware of the connectedness of life. His corn cannot improve unless his neighbor's corn also improves.

So it is with our lives. Those who choose to live in peace must help their neighbors to live in peace. Those who choose to live well must help others to live well, for the value of a life is measured by the lives it touches. And those who choose to be happy must help others to find happiness, for the welfare of each is bound up with the welfare of all.

The lesson for each of us is this: if we are to grow good corn, we must help our neighbors grow good corn.

It is possible to give away and become richer! It is also possible to hold on too tightly and lose everything. Yes, the generous man shall be rich! By watering others, he waters himself.

The Lion and The cougar

A pointed fable is told about a young lion and a cougar. Both thirsty, the animals arrived at their usual water hole at the same time. They immediately began to argue about who should satisfy their thirst first. The argument became heated, and each decided he would rather die than give up the privilege of being first to quench his thirst.

As they stubbornly confronted each other, their emotions turned to rage. Their cruel attacks on each other were suddenly interrupted. They both looked up. Circling overhead was a flock of vultures waiting for the loser to fall. Quietly, the two beasts turned and walked away. The thought of being devoured was all they needed to end their quarrel.

The King And His Horseman

A long time ago, there was an Emperor who told his horseman that if he could ride on his horse and cover as much land area as he likes, then the Emperor would give him the area of land he has covered.

Sure enough, the horseman quickly jumped onto his horse and rode as fast as possible to cover as much land area as he could. He kept on riding and riding, whipping the horse to go as fast as possible. When he was hungry or tired, he did not stop because he wanted to cover as much area as possible.

At some point he had covered a substantial area but he was so exhausted and dehydrated that he was on the verge of dying.

While taking his last breath he thought to himself, "Why did I push myself so hard to cover so much land area? Now I am dying and all I need is a small area to be buried in."

The above story reflects the journey of our Life. We push ourselves hard every day to make more money, to gain more power and recognition, while sometimes neglecting our health, time with our family and the appreciation of the beauty that surrounds us.

One day we may look back and realize that we don't really need that much, but then we cannot turn back time for what we have missed.

Island Of Feelings

Once upon a time there was an island where all the feelings lived together.

One day there was a storm in the sea and the island was about to get drowned. Every feeling was scared but love made a boat to escape. Every feeling boarded the boat.

Only one feeling was left. Love got down to see who was it... It was EGO... LOVE tried and tried but ego wasn't moving, meantime the water was rising. Every one asked Love to leave him and come to the boat, but Love was made to Love.

At last all the feelings escapes and LOVE dies with EGO on the island.

LOVE dies because of EGO. So, kill EGO and save LOVE...

The Governor's Wife

There is a cute story told about the Governor of Texas, then Mark White.

Governor White and his wife were driving through the open Texas countryside one day, out for a relaxing drive and talk.

The couple happened to be around the area where Mrs. White grew up, and as they pulled into a gas station to fuel up and check out the car, Mark noticed a little nervousness with his wife.

He didn't say anything, but when the gas station attendant came out to their car, Mark began to notice what was really going on. Both his wife and the attendant looked surprised to see each other, and they acted with that awkwardness that two people have when they've been close in the past, but weren't anymore.

Governor White pretended not to notice this. They finished at the gas station and continued back down the highway. The car fell silent and neither said a word. For a long time they remained silent, and all the while Mrs. White kept looking out the window, staring off out into the distance.

Mark was considerate and patient with this silence, and he continued to drive in the silence. But after the silence had gone on for almost an hour, he interrupted, trying to break the silence.

"Honey, I couldn't help but notice how you and that gas station attendant looked at each other. You were involved with each other at one point, weren't you," he asked ?

"Well, yea," She responded, quietly.

"Well, I guess I know how you feel. You were probably thinking about that and needed some space, right?" He continued.

"Yea," she said again.

"I guess you were probably thinking about how different your two lives had become. I guess you were thinking that if you had married him, then you'd be the wife of a gas station attendant now, instead of my wife. Right?" he said.

"Well, No. Actually I was thinking that he'd be the governor now."

Enjoy Your Coffee

A Group of friends, highly established in their careers, got together to visit their old university professor. Conversation soon turned into complaints about stress in work and life.

Offering his guests coffee, the professor went to the kitchen and returned with a large pot of coffee and assortment of cups – porcelain, plastic, glass, crystal, some plain looking, some expensive, some exquisite – telling them to help themselves to the coffee.

When all the students had a cup of coffee in hand, the professor said: "If you noticed, all the nice looking expensive cups were taken up, leaving behind the plain and cheap ones. While it is normal for you to want only the best for yourselves, that is the source of problems and stress. Be assured that the cup itself adds no quality to the coffee. In most cases it is just more expensive and in some cases even hides what we drink. What all of you really wanted was coffee, not the cup, but you consciously went for the best cups... And then began envying each other's cups.

Now consider this: "Life is the COFFEE; the jobs, money and position in the society are the CUPS. They are just tools to hold and contain Life, and the type of cup we have does not define, nor change the quality of Life we live. Sometimes, by concentrating only on the cup, we fail to enjoy the coffee".

The happiest people don't necessarily have the best of everything. They just make the best of everything. Live simply. Love generously. Care deeply. Speak kindly.

Enjoy your coffee...

The House With The Golden Windows

The little girl lived in a small, very simple, poor house on a hill and she would play in the small garden. As she grew up she was able to see over the garden fence and across the valley to a wonderful house high on the hill – and this house had golden windows, so golden and shining that the little girl would dream of how magic it would be to grow up and live in a house with golden windows instead of an ordinary house like hers.

And although she loved her parents and her family, she yearned to live in such a golden house and dreamed all day about how wonderful and exciting it must feel to live there.

When she got to an age where she gained enough skill and responsibility to go outside her garden fence, she asked her mother if she could go for a bike ride outside the gate and down the lane. After pleading her mother finally allowed her to go, insisting that she kept close to the house and didn't wander too far.

The day was beautiful and the little girl knew exactly where she was heading! Down the lane and across the valley, she rode her bike until she got to the gate of the golden house across the other hill.

As she parked her bike and lent it against the gate, she focused her eyes on the path that lead to the house and then on the house itself...and was so disappointed as she realized that all the windows were plain and rather dirty, reflecting nothing other than the sad neglect of the house that stood derelict.

She was so sad that she didn't go any further and turned, heartbroken. As she remounted her bike and glanced up she saw a sight to amazed her... There across the way on her side of the valley was a little house and its windows sparkled golden... As the sun shone on her little home.

She then realized that she had been living in her golden house and all the love and care she found there was what made her home the 'golden house'. Everything she dreamed of was right there in front of her nose!

To Build a Bridge

The Brooklyn Bridge that spans the river tying Manhattan Island to Brooklyn is truly a miracle bridge. In 1863, a creative engineer named John Roebling was inspired by an idea for this spectacular bridge. However, bridge-building experts throughout the world told him to forget it; it could not be done.

Roebling convinced his son, Washington, who was a young up and coming engineer, that the bridge could be built. The two of them developed the concepts of how it could be accomplished and how the obstacles could be overcome. With an un harnessed excitement and inspiration, they hired their crew and began to build their dream bridge.

The project was only a few months under construction when a tragic accident on the site took the life of John Roebling and severely injured his son, Washington. Washington was left with permanent brain damage and was unable to talk or walk. Everyone felt that the project would have to be scrapped since the Roeblings were the only ones who knew how the bridge could be built.

Even though Washington was unable to move or talk, his mind was as sharp as ever, and he still had a burning desire to complete the bridge. An idea hit him as he lay in his hospital bed, and he developed a code for communication. All he could move was one finger, so he touched the arm of his wife with that finger, tapping out the code to communicate to her what to tell the engineers who were building the bridge. For thirteen years, Washington tapped out his instructions with his finger until the spectacular Brooklyn Bridge was finally completed.

A $1.11 Miracle (True Story!)

Tess was a precocious eight year old when she heard her Mom and Dad talking about her little brother, Andrew. All she knew was that he was very sick and they were completely out of money.

They were moving to a rental apartment complex next month because Daddy didn't have the money for the doctor bills and their house. Only a very costly surgery could save him now and it was looking like there was no-one to loan them the money. She heard Daddy say to her tearful Mother with whispered desperation, "Only a miracle can save him now."

Tess went to her bedroom and pulled a glass jelly jar from its hiding place in the closet. She poured all the change out on the floor and counted it carefully. Three times, even. The total had to be exactly perfect. No chance here for mistakes.

Carefully placing the coins back in the jar and twisting on the cap, she slipped out the back door and made her way 6 blocks to Rexall's Drug Store with the big red Indian Chief sign above the door.

She waited patiently for the pharmacist to give her some attention but he was too busy at this moment. Tess twisted her feet to make a scuffing noise. Nothing. She cleared her throat with the most disgusting sound she could muster. No good.

Finally she took a quarter from her jar and banged it on the glass counter. That did it!

"And what do you want?" the pharmacist asked in an annoyed tone of voice. "I'm talking to my brother from Chicago whom I haven't seen in ages,"He said without waiting for a reply to his question.

"Well, I want to talk to you about my brother," Tess answered back in the same annoyed tone. "He's really, really sick… and I want to buy a miracle."

"I beg your pardon?" said the pharmacist.

"His name is Andrew and he has something bad growing inside his head and my Daddy says only a miracle can save him now. So how much does a miracle cost?"

"We don't sell miracles here, little girl. I'm sorry but I can't help you," the pharmacist said, softening a little. "Listen, I have the money to pay for it. If it isn't enough, I will get the rest. Just tell me how much it costs."

The pharmacist's brother was a well dressed man. He stooped down and asked the little girl, "What kind of a miracle does your brother need?"

"I don't know," Tess replied with her eyes welling up. "I just know he's really sick and Mommy says he needs an operation. But my Daddy can't pay for it, so I want to use my money."

"How much do you have?" asked the man from Chicago. "One dollar and eleven cents," Tess answered barely audibly. "And it's all the money I have, but I can get some more if I need to."

"Well, what a coincidence," smiled the man. "A dollar and eleven cents – the exact price of a miracle for little brothers." He took her money in one hand and with the other hand he grasped her mitten and said, "Take me to where you live. I want to see your brother and meet your parents. Let's see if I have the kind of miracle you need."

That well dressed man was Dr. Carlton Armstrong, a surgeon, specializing in neuro-surgery. The operation was completed without charge and it wasn't long until Andrew was home again and doing well. Mom and Dad were happily talking about the chain of events that had led them to this place.

"That surgery," her Mom whispered. "was a real miracle. I wonder how much it would have cost?"

Tess smiled. She knew exactly how much a miracle cost… one dollar and eleven cents … plus the faith of a little child.

Chance Encounter

Mark was walking home from school one day when he noticed the boy ahead of him had tripped and dropped all of the books he was carrying, along with two sweaters, a baseball bat, a glove and a small tape recorder.

Mark knelt down and helped the boy pick up the scattered articles. Since they were going the same way, he helped to carry part of the burden. As they walked Mark discovered the boy's name was Bill, that he loved video games, baseball and history, and that he was having lots of trouble with his other subjects and that he had just broken up with his girlfriend. They arrived at Bill's home first and Mark was invited in for a Coke and to watch some television. The afternoon passed pleasantly with a few laughs and some shared small talk, then Mark went home.

They continued to see each other around school, had lunch together once or twice, then both graduated from junior high school. They ended up in the same high school where they had brief contacts over the years. Finally the long awaited senior year came and three weeks before graduation, Bill asked Mark if they could talk.

Bill reminded him of the day years ago when they had first met. "Did you ever wonder why I was carrying so many things home that day?" asked Bill. "You see, I cleaned out my locker because I didn't want to leave a mess for anyone else. I had stored away some of my mother's sleeping pills and I was going home to commit suicide. But after we spent some time together talking and laughing, I realized that if I had killed myself, I would have missed that time and so many others that might follow. So you see, Mark, when you picked up those books that day, you did a lot more, you saved my life."

True Friend

Horror gripped the heart of the World War I soldier as he saw his lifelong friend fall in battle. Caught in a trench with continuous gunfire whizzing over his head, the soldier asked his lieutenant if he might go out into the "no man's land" between the trenches to bring his fallen comrade back.

"You can go," said the lieutenant, "But I don't think it will be worth it. Your friend is probably dead and you may throw your life away." The lieutenant's advice didn't matter, and the soldier went anyway. Miraculously he managed to reach his friend, hoist him onto his shoulder and bring him back to their company's trench. As the two of them tumbled in together to the bottom of the trench, the officer checked the wounded soldier, and then looked kindly at his friend.

"I told you it wouldn't be worth it," he said. "Your friend is dead and you are mortally wounded."

"It was worth it, though, sir," said the soldier.

"What do you mean; worth it?" responded the Lieutenant. "Your friend is dead."

"Yes, Sir" the private answered. "But it was worth it because when I got to him, he was still alive and I had the satisfaction of hearing him saying, "Jim…, I knew you'd come."

Many times in life, whether a thing is worth doing or not really depends on how you looks at it. Take up all your courage and do something your heart tells you to do so that you may not regret not doing it later in your life. May each and every one of you be blessed with the company of true friends. A true friend is one who walks in, when the rest of the world walks out. War doesn't determine who's right. War only determines who's left.

A Salty Coffee

He met her at a party. She was so outstanding, many guys chasing after her, while he was so normal, nobody paid attention to him. At the end of the party, he invited her to have coffee with him, she was surprised but out of politeness she agreed. They sat in a nice coffee shop, he was too nervous to say anything, she felt uncomfortable, and she thought to herself, "Please, let me go home..."

Suddenly he asked the waiter, "Would you please bring me some salt? I'd like to put it in my coffee." Everybody stared at him, so strange! His face turned red but still, he put the salt in his coffee and drank it. She asked him curiously, "How come you drink your coffee with salt?" He replied, "When I was a little boy, I lived near the sea, I liked playing in the sea, I could feel the taste of the sea, just like the taste of the salty coffee. Now every time I have the salty coffee, It reminds me of my childhood, of my hometown, I miss my hometown so much, I miss my parents who are still living there." While saying that tears filled his eyes. She was deeply touched.

That's his true feeling, from the bottom of his heart. A man who can tell out his homesickness, he must be a man who loves home, cares about family and home... Then she also started to open up, spoke about her faraway hometown, her childhood, her family.

That was a really nice talk, also a beautiful beginning of their story. They continued to date. She found that actually he was a man who meets all her wishes; he had tolerance, was kind hearted, warm, careful.

He was such a good person and she almost missed him! Thanks to his salty coffee she didn't!

Then the story was just like every beautiful love story, the princess married the prince, and they were living the happy life... And every time she made coffee for him, she didn't forget to put some salt in it, as she knew that's the way he liked it.

After 40 years, he passed away, left her a letter which said, "My dearest, please forgive me, forgive my whole life's lie. This was the only lie I said to you - the salty coffee. Remember the first time we dated? I was so nervous at that time, actually I wanted some sugar, but I said salt. I was too embarrassed to change so I just went ahead. I never thought that could be the start of our communication!

I tried to tell you the truth many times during our life, but I was too afraid to do that, as I have promised not to lie to you for anything... Now I'm dying, I afraid of nothing so I'm telling you the truth, I don't like salty coffee, what a strange bad taste... But I have had the salty coffee for my whole life!

Having you with me has been my biggest happiness. If I could live for a second time, I would still want to know you and spend my whole life with you, even though I have to drink the salty coffee again." Her tears made the letter totally wet.

Someday, someone asked her, "What's the taste of salty coffee?" She replied, "It's sweet."

Spoken Words Can't Be Retrieved

A farmer insulted his neighbor. Realizing his mistake, he went to the preacher to ask for forgiveness. The preacher told him to take a bag of feathers and drop them in the center of the town.

The farmer did as he was told. Then the preacher asked him to go and collect the feathers and put them back in the bag.

The farmer tried but couldn't as the feathers had all blown away. When he returned with the empty bag, the preacher said, "The same thing is true about your words. You dropped them rather easily but you cannot retrieve them, so be very careful in choosing your words."

Shake Off Your Problems

One day a farmer's donkey fell down into a well. The animal cried piteously for hours as the farmer tried to figure out what to do. Finally, he decided the animal was old, and the well needed to be covered up anyway; it just wasn't worth it to retrieve the donkey.

He invited all his neighbors to come over and help him. They all grabbed a shovel and began to shovel dirt into the well. At first, the donkey realized what was happening and cried horribly. Then, to everyone's amazement he quieted down.

A few shovel loads later, the farmer finally looked down the well. He was astonished at what he saw. With each shovel of dirt that hit his back, the donkey was doing something amazing. He would shake it off and take a step up.

As the farmer's neighbors continued to shovel dirt on top of the animal, he would shake it off and take a step up. Pretty soon, everyone was amazed as the donkey stepped up over the edge of the well and happily trotted off!

Moral: Life is going to shovel dirt on you, all kinds of dirt. The trick to getting out of the well is to shake it off and take a step up. Each of our troubles is a steppingstone. We can get out of the deepest wells just by not stopping, never giving up! Shake it off and take a step up.

Remember the four simple rules to be happy:

1. Free your heart from hatred - Forgive.

2. Free your mind from worries - Most never happens.

3. Live simply and appreciate what you have.

4. Give more.

Making A Small Difference

There was a man taking a morning walk at the beach. He saw that along with the morning tide came hundreds of starfish and when the tide receded, they were left behind and with the morning sun rays, they would die.

The tide was fresh and the starfish were alive. The man took a few steps, picked one and threw it into the water. He did that repeatedly.

Right behind him there was another person who couldn't understand what this man was doing. He caught up with him and asked, "What are you doing? There are hundreds of starfish. How many can you help? What difference does it make?"

This man did not reply, took two more steps, picked up another one, threw it into the water, and said, "It makes a difference to this one."

What difference are we making? Big or small, it does not matter. If everyone made a small difference, we'd end up with a big difference, wouldn't we?

Law Of The Garbage Truck

Recently I hopped in a Taxi and we took off for the Airport. We were driving in the right lane when suddenly a black car jumped out of a parking space right in front of us.

My taxi driver slammed on his brakes, skidded, and missed the other car by just inches!

The driver of the other car whipped his head around and started yelling at us. My taxi driver just smiled and waved at the guy. And I mean, he was really friendly.

So I asked, 'Why did you just do that? This guy almost ruined your car and sent us to the hospital!'

This is when my Taxi driver taught me what I now call, 'The Law of the Garbage Truck'

He explained that many people are like garbage trucks. They run around full of garbage, full of frustration, full of anger, and full of disappointment. As their garbage piles up, they need a place to dump it and sometimes they'll dump it on you. Don't take it personally.

Just smile, wave, wish them well, and move on. Don't take their garbage and spread it to other people at work, at home, or on the streets. The bottom line is that successful people do not let Garbage Trucks take over their day.

Life's too short to wake up in the morning with regrets, so... Love the people who treat you right. Pray for the ones who don't.

Life is Ten percent what you make of it and Ninety percent how you take it!

Have a garbage-free day.

Life Is Full Of Imperfect Things

When I was a kid, my Mom liked to make breakfast food for dinner every now and then and I remember one night in particular when she had made breakfast after a long, hard day at work.

On that evening so long ago, my Mom placed a plate of eggs, sausage and extremely burnt biscuits in front of my dad. I remember waiting to see if anyone noticed!

Yet all my dad did was reach for the biscuit, smile at my Mom and ask me how my day was at school. I don't remember what I told him that night, but I do remember hearing my Mom apologize to my dad for burning the biscuits. And I'll never forget what he said: "Honey, I love burned biscuits".

"Later that night I went to kiss my Daddy good night and I asked him if he really liked his biscuits burned. He wrapped me in his arms and said, "Your momma put in a long hard day at work today and she is realy tired. And besides... A burnt biscuit never hurt anyone!".

You know, life is full of imperfect things... And imperfect people. I'm not the best at hardly anything and I forget birthdays and anniversaries just like everyone. What I have learned over the years is that learning to accept each other's faults and choosing to celebrate each other's differences is one of the most important key to creating a healthy, growing, and lasting relationship. So... please pass me a biscuit. And yes, the burnt one will just do fine.

Life is too short to wake up with regrets... love the people who treat you right and have compassion for the ones who don't. Enjoy life now – It as an expiration date!

A True Love Story

One day, a young guy and a young girl fell in love. But the guy came from a poor family. The girl's parents weren't too happy.

So the young man decided not only to court the girl but to court her parents as well. In time, the parents saw that he was a good man and was worthy of their daughter's hand.

But there was another problem: The man was a soldier. Soon war broke out and he was being sent overseas for a year. The week before he left, the man knelt on his knee and asked his lady love, "Will you marry me?" She wiped a tear, said yes, and they were engaged. They agreed that when he got back in one year, they would get married.

But tragedy struck. A few days after he left, the girl had a major vehicular accident. It was a head-on collision.

When she woke up in the hospital, she saw her father and mother crying. Immediately, she knew there was something wrong.

She later found out that she suffered a brain injury. The part of her brain that controlled her face muscles was damaged. Her once lovely face was now disfigured. She cried as she saw herself in the mirror. "Yesterday, I was beautiful. Today, I'm a monster." Her body was also covered with so many ugly wounds.

Right there and then, she decided to release her fiancé from their promise. She knew he wouldn't want her anymore. She would forget about him and never see him again.

For one year, the soldier wrote many letters - but she wouldn't answer. He phoned her many times but she wouldn't return her calls.

But after one year, the mother walked into her room and announced, "He's back from the war."

The girl shouted, "No! Please don't tell him about me. Don't tell him I'm here!"

The mother said, "He's getting married," and handed her a wedding invitation.

The girl's heart sank. She knew she still loved him - but she had to forget him now.

With great sadness, she opened the wedding invitation. And then she saw her name on it!

Confused, she asked, "What is this?"

That was when the young man entered her room with a bouquet of flowers. He knelt beside her and asked, "Will you marry me?"

The girl covered her face with her hands and said, "I'm ugly!"

The man said, "Without your permission, your mother sent me your photos. When I saw your photos, I realized that nothing has changed. You're still the person I fell in love with. You're still as beautiful as ever. Because I love you!"

Spend Time With Your Family

A man narrating his date with his mother after 21 years...

After 21 years of marriage, my wife wanted me to take another woman out to dinner and a movie. She said, "I love you, but I know this other woman loves you and would love to spend some time with you."

The other woman that my wife wanted me to visit was my mother, who has been a widow for 19 years, but the demands of my work and my three children had made it possible to visit her only occasionally. That night I called to invite her to go out for dinner and a movie. "What's wrong, are you well?" she asked.

My mother is the type of woman who suspects that a late night call or a surprise invitation is a sign of bad news. "I thought that it would be pleasant to spend some time with you," I responded. "Just the two of us." She thought about it for a moment, and then said, "I would like that very much."

That Friday after work, as I drove over to pick her up I was a bit nervous. When I arrived at her house, I noticed that she, too, seemed to be nervous about our date. She waited in the door with her coat on. She had curled her hair and was wearing the dress that she had worn to celebrate her last wedding anniversary. She smiled from a face that was as radiant as an angel's. "I told my friends that I was going to go out with my son, and they were impressed," she said, as she got into the car. "They can't wait to hear about our meeting."

We went to a restaurant that, although not elegant, was very nice and cozy. My mother took my arm as if she were the First Lady. After we sat down, I had to read the menu. Her eyes could only read large print. Half way through the entries, I lifted my eyes and saw Mom sitting there staring at me. A nostalgic smile was on her lips. "It was I who used to have to read the menu when you were small," she said. "Then it's time that you relax and let me return the favor," I responded. During the dinner, we had an agreeable conversation – nothing extraordinary but catching up on recent events of each other's life. We talked so much that we missed the movie. As we arrived at her house later, she said, "I'll go out with you again, but only if you let me invite you." I agreed.

"How was your dinner date?" asked my wife when I got home. "Very nice. Much more so than I could have imagined," I answered.

A few days later, my mother died of a massive heart attack, It happened so suddenly that I didn't have a chance to do anything for her. Sometime later, I received an envelope with a copy of a restaurant receipt from the same place mother and I had dined. An attached note said: "I paid this bill in advance. I wasn't sure that I could be there; but nevertheless, I paid for two plates – one for you and the other for your wife. You will never know what that night meant for me. I love you, son."

At that moment, I understood the importance of saying in time: "I Love You" and to give our loved ones the time that they deserve.

Nothing in life is more important than your family. Give them the time they deserve, because these things cannot be put off till some other time.

"I Am Sorry"

Once there was a man who had 3 daughters and was a single parent to his children.

One morning he asked his oldest daughter, Sonia, to do the breakfast dishes before going to school. Not realizing that she was already running late and facing too many tardy notices, he was stunned by her reaction. She burst into profuse tears.

Again, misinterpreting the motive behind the outburst, assuming that she was merely trying to get out of an unpleasant chore, he demanded that she dry her tears and get back to work immediately.

She reluctantly obeyed him, but her anger could be clearly heard in the careless clanking of the dishes in the sink, she turned back to her father and stared sullenly out the window.

Usually the man used to take advantage of the uninterrupted time to spend with his children while driving them to school by teaching poetry. However that morning there was no poetry - only deathly, stubborn silence.

The man dropped his daughter, mumbled a good bye and moved to his office. He tried to work but couldn't concentrate, all he could see was his daughter's scared, tear-stained face as she hesitantly climbed out of the car to face her teachers and classmates.

The man began to realize that his timing had gone wrong and with the passage of the day he began to feel remorseful. So he decided to say 'sorry' to his daughter and couldn't wait till lunch to apologize.

So he got permission from the school to take his daughter for lunch and was astonished to see the surprise on her face. He led her by her arm through the corridor and as the doors banged behind them, he turned towards his daughter and said, "Sonia, I am sorry. I am so very sorry! It's not that I shouldn't have asked you to help out at home, but I had no right to do it on this morning. I upset you at a time when you most needed my love and support - just before you went to school. And I let you go without saying 'I love you'. I was wrong. Please forgive me."

Sonia put her arms around her father's neck and hugged him and said "Oh, Dad, of course I forgive you. I love you too."

The power of these restorative words, "I am Sorry!" is such that they heal relationships – between us and our friends and loved ones.

God's Days

There are two days in the week upon which and about which I never worry -- two carefree days kept sacredly free from fear and apprehension. One of these days is Yesterday. Yesterday, with its cares and fret and pains and aches, all its faults, its mistakes and blunders, has passed forever beyond my recall. It was mine; it is God's.

The other day that I do not worry about is Tomorrow. Tomorrow, with all its possible adversities, its burdens, its perils, its large promise and performance, its failures and mistakes, is as far beyond my mastery as its dead sister, Yesterday. Tomorrow is God's day; it will be mine.

There is left, then, for myself but one day in the week - Today. Any man can fight the battles of today. Any woman can carry the burdens of just one day; any man can resist the temptation of today. It is only when we willfully add the burden of these two awful eternities - Yesterday and Tomorrow - such burdens as only the Mighty God can sustain - that we break down.

It isn't the experience of Today that drives men mad. It is the remorse of what happened Yesterday and fear of what Tomorrow might bring. These are God's Days ... Leave them to Him.

The Triple Filter Test

In ancient Greece, Socrates was reputed to hold knowledge in high esteem. One day an acquaintance met the great philosopher and said, "Do you know what I just heard about your friend?"

"Hold on a minute," Socrates replied. "Before you talk to me about my friend, it might be good idea to take a moment and filter what you're going to say. That's why I call it the triple filter test. The first filter is Truth. Have you made absolutely sure that what you are about to tell me is true?"

"Well, no," the man said, "actually I just heard about it and…"

"All right," said Socrates. "So you don't really know if it's true or not. Now, let's try the second filter, the filter of Goodness. Is what you are about to tell me about my friend something good?"

"Umm, no, on the contrary…"

"So," Socrates continued, "you want to tell me something bad about my friend, but you're not certain it's true. You may still pass the test though, because there's one filter left—the filter of Usefulness. Is what you want to tell me about my friend going to be useful to me?"

"No, not really."

"Well," concluded Socrates, "if what you want to tell me is

neither true, nor good, nor even useful, why tell it to me at all?"

Reaction vs. Response

Suddenly, a cockroach flew from somewhere and sat on her. I wondered if this was the cockroach's response to all the glory that was spoken about it! She started screaming out of fear. With panic stricken face and trembling voice, she started doing jumping, with both her hands desperately trying to get rid of the cockroach. Her reaction was contagious, as everyone in her group got cranky to what was happening.

The lady finally managed to push the cockroach to another lady in the group. Now, it was the turn of the other lady in the group to continue the drama. The waitress rushed forward to their rescue. In the relay of throwing, the cockroach next fell upon the waitress.

The waitress stood firm, composed herself and observed the behavior of the cockroach on her shirt. When she was confident enough, she grabbed and threw it out with her fingers.

Sipping my coffee and watching the amusement, the antenna of my mind picked up a few thoughts and started wondering, was the cockroach responsible for their hysteric behavior? If so, then why was the waitress not disturbed? she handled it near to perfection, without any chaos. It is not the cockroach, but the inability of the ladies to handle the disturbance caused by the cockroach that disturbed the ladies.

I realized even in my case then, it is not the shouting of my father or my boss that disturbs me, but it's my inability to handle the disturbances caused by their shouting that disturbs me.

It's not the traffic jams on the road that disturbs me, but my inability to handle the disturbance caused by the traffic jam that disturbs me.

More than the problem, it's my reaction to the problem that hurts me.

Lessons learnt from the story:

I understood, I should not react in life. I should always respond.

The women reacted, whereas the waitress responded.

Reactions are always instinctive whereas responses are always intellectual...

The Frog In A Milk Pail

A frog was hopping around a farmyard, when it decided to investigate the barn. Being somewhat careless, and maybe a little too curious, he ended up falling into a pail half-filled with fresh milk.

As he swam about attempting to reach the top of the pail, he found that the sides of the pail were too high and steep to reach. He tried to stretch his back legs to push off the bottom of the pail but found it too deep. But this frog was determined not to give up, and he continued to struggle.

He kicked and squirmed and kicked and squirmed, until at last, all his churning about in the milk had turned the milk into a big hunk of butter. The butter was now solid enough for him to climb onto and get out of the pail!

The moral of the story? Never Give Up!

Building Bridges

Once upon a time two brothers who lived on adjoining farms fell into conflict. It was the first serious rift in 40 years of farming side by side, sharing machinery, and trading labor and goods as needed without a hitch.

Then the long collaboration fell apart. It began with a small misunderstanding and it grew into a major difference, and finally it exploded into an exchange of bitter words followed by weeks of silence.

One morning there was a knock on John's door. He opened it to find a man with a carpenter's toolbox. "I'm looking for a few days work," he said.

"Perhaps you would have a few small jobs here and there. Could I help you?"

"Yes," said the older brother. "I do have a job for you. Look across the creek at that farm. That's my neighbor, in fact, it's my younger brother. Last week there was a meadow between us and he took his bulldozer to the river levee and now there is a creek between us. Well, he may have done this to spite me, but I'll go him one better. See that pile of lumber curing by the barn? I want you to build me a fence - an 8-foot fence - so I won't need to see his place anymore. Cool him down, anyhow."

The carpenter said, "I think I understand the situation. Show me the nails and the post-hole digger and I'll be able to do a job that pleases you."

The older brother had to go to town for supplies, so he helped the carpenter get the materials ready and then he was off for the day.

The carpenter worked hard all that day measuring, sawing, nailing.

About sunset when the farmer returned, the carpenter had just finished his job. The farmer's eyes opened wide, his jaw dropped.

There was no fence there at all. It was a bridge... a bridge stretching from one side of the creek to the other! A fine piece of work handrails and all - and the neighbor, his younger brother, was coming across, his hand outstretched.

"You are quite a fellow to build this bridge after all I've said and done."

The two brothers stood at each end of the bridge, and then they met in the middle, taking each other's hand. They turned to see the carpenter hoist his toolbox on his shoulder. "No, wait! Stay a few days. I've a lot of other projects for you," said the older brother.

"I'd love to stay on," the carpenter said, "but, I have many more bridges to build."

Meaningless Goals

A farmer had a dog who used to sit by the roadside waiting for vehicles to come around. As soon as one came he would run down the road, barking and trying to overtake it.

One day a neighbor asked the farmer "Do you think your dog is ever going to catch a car?" The farmer replied, "That is not what bothers me. What bothers me is what he would do if he ever caught one."

Many people in life behave just like that dog who is pursuing meaningless goals.

A Box Full of Kisses

Some time ago, a man punished his 3-year-old daughter for wasting a roll of gold wrapping paper. Money was tight and he became infuriated when the child tried to decorate a box to put under the Christmas tree.

Nevertheless, the little girl brought the gift to her father the next morning and said, "This is for you, Daddy."

The man became embarrassed by his overreaction earlier, but his rage continue when he saw that the box was empty. He yelled at her; "Don't you know, when you give someone a present, there is supposed to be something inside?"

The little girl looked up at him with tears in her eyes and cried;

"Oh, Daddy, it's not empty at all. I blew kisses into the box. They're all for you, Daddy."

The father was crushed. He put his arms around his little girl, and begged for her forgiveness.

Only a short time later, an accident took the life of the child. Her father kept the gold box by his bed for many years and, whenever he was discouraged, he would take out an imaginary kiss and remember the love of the child who had put it there.

Moral of the story: Love is the most precious gift in the world.

Puppies for Sale

A shop owner placed a sign above his door that said: "Puppies For Sale."

Signs like this always have a way of attracting young children, and to no surprise, a boy saw the sign and approached the owner; "How much are you going to sell the puppies for?" he asked.

The store owner replied, "Anywhere from $30 to $50."

The little boy pulled out some change from his pocket. "I only have $2.37," he said. "Can I please look at them?"

The shop owner smiled and whistled. Out of the kennel came a Lady, who ran down the aisle of his shop followed by five teeny, tiny balls of fur. One puppy was lagging considerably behind. Immediately the little boy singled out the lagging, limping puppy and said, "What's wrong with that little dog?"

The shop owner explained that the veterinarian had examined the little puppy and had discovered it didn't have a hip socket. It would always limp. It would always be lame.

The little boy became excited. "That is the puppy that I want to buy."

The shop owner said, "No, you don't want to buy that little dog. If you really want him, I'll just give him to you."

The little boy got quite upset. He looked straight into the store owner's eyes, pointing his finger, and said;

"I don't want you to give him to me. That little dog is worth every bit as much as all the other dogs and I'll pay full price. In fact, I'll give you $2.37 now, and 50 cents a month until I have him paid for."

The shop owner countered, "You really don't want to buy this little dog. He is never going to be able to run and jump and play with you like the other puppies."

To his surprise, the little boy reached down and rolled up his pant leg to reveal a badly twisted, crippled left leg supported by a big metal brace. He looked up at the shop owner and softly replied, "Well, I don't run so well myself, and the little puppy will need someone who understands!"

Who's Counting?

Napoleon was involved in conversation with a colonel of a Hungarian battalion who had been taken prisoner in Italy. The colonel mentioned he had fought in the army of Maria Theresa. "You must have a few years under your belt!" exclaimed Napoleon. "I'm sure I've lived sixty or seventy years," replied the colonel. "You mean to say," Napoleon continued, "you have not kept track of the years you have lived?"

To that the colonel promptly replied, "Sir, I always count my money, my shirts, and my horses - but as for my years, I know nobody who wants to steal them, and I shall surely never lose them."

Control Your Temper

There once was a little boy who had a very bad temper. His father decided to hand him a bag of nails and said that every time the boy lost his temper, he had to hammer a nail into the fence.

On the first day, the boy hammered 37 nails into that fence. The boy gradually began to control his temper over the next few weeks, and number of nails he was hammering into the fence slowly decreased. He discovered it was easier to control his temper than to hammer those nails into the fence.

Finally, the day came when the boy didn't lose his temper at all. He told his father the news and the father suggested that the boy should now pull out a nail every day he kept his temper under control.

The days passed and the young boy was finally able to tell his father that all the nails were gone. The father took his son by the hand and led him to the fence.

"you have done well, my son, but look at the holes in the fence. The fence will never be the same. When you say things in anger, they leave a scar just like this one. You can put a knife in a man and draw it out. It won't matter how many times you say I'm sorry, the wound is still there."

Moral of the story: Control your anger, and don't say things to people in the heat of the moment that you may later regret. Some things in life, you are unable to take back.

The Butterfly

A man found a cocoon of a butterfly, he took it home and put it in a jar. One day a small opening appeared. He sat and watched the butterfly for several hours as it struggled to force its body through that little hole. Until it suddenly stopped making any progress, and looked like it was stuck.

So the man decided to help the butterfly. He took a pair of scissors and snipped off the remaining bit of the cocoon.

The butterfly then emerged easily, although it had a swollen body and small, shriveled wings.

The man didn't think anything of it, and sat there waiting for the wings to enlarge to support the butterfly. But that didn't happen. The butterfly spent the rest of its life unable to fly, crawling around with tiny wings and a swollen body.

Despite the kind heart of the man, he didn't understand that the restricting cocoon and the struggle needed by the butterfly to get itself through the small opening were Natures way of forcing fluid from the body of the butterfly into its wings to prepare itself for flying once it was out of the cocoon.

Moral of the story: Our struggles in life develop our strengths. Without struggles we never grow and never get stronger, so it's important for us to tackle challenges on our own, and not just wait and rely on help from others.

Fear And Loathing in The Gym

Dear Diary,

For my 50th birthday, my husband, the dear, purchased a week of personal training at the local health club for me.

Although I am still in great shape since playing on my high school softball team, I decided it would be a good idea to go ahead and give it a try.

I called the club and made my reservations with a personal trainer I'll call Bruce, who identified himself as a 26 year old aerobics instructor and model for athletic clothing and swim wear.

My husband seemed pleased with my enthusiasm to get started. The club encouraged me to keep this diary to chart my progress...

Monday : Started my day at 6:00 a.m. Tough to get out of bed, but found it was well worth the effort when I arrived at the health club and found Bruce waiting for me. He is something of a Greek God! with blonde hair, dancing blue eyes and a dazzling white smile. Woo Hoo!!!

Bruce gave me a tour and showed me the machines. He took my pulse after five minutes on the treadmill. He was alarmed that my pulse was so fast, but I attribute it to standing next to him in his Lycra aerobic outfit. I enjoyed watching the skillful way in which he conducted his aerobics class after my workout today. Very inspiring!

Bruce was encouraging as I did my sit-ups, although my gut was already aching from holding it in the whole time he was around. This is going to be a FANTASTIC week!

Tuesday: I drank a whole pot of coffee, but I finally made it out the door. Bruce made me lie on my back and push a heavy iron bar into the air, then he put weights on it! My legs were a little wobbly on the treadmill, but I made the full mile. Bruce's rewarding smile made it all worthwhile. I feel GREAT!! It's a whole new life for me!!!

Wednesday: The only way I can brush my teeth is by laying on the toothbrush on the counter and moving my mouth back and forth over it. I believe I have a hernia in both pectorals. Driving was OK as long as I didn't try to steer or to stop. I parked on top of a GEO in the club parking lot. Bruce was impatient with me, insisting that my screams bothered the other club members. His voice is a little too perky for early in the morning and when he scolds he gets this nasally whine that is VERY annoying. My chest hurt when I got on the treadmill, so Bruce put me on the stair monster. Why the heck would anyone invent a machine to simulate an activity rendered obsolete by elevators? Bruce told me it would help me get in shape and enjoy life. He said some other useless sh** too!

Thursday: Bruce was waiting for me with his vampire-like teeth exposed as his thin, cruel lips were pulled back in a full snarl. I couldn't help being half an hour late, it took me that long to tie my shoes! Bruce took me to work out with dumbbells. When he was not looking, I ran and hid in the men's room. He sent Lars in to find me, then, as punishment, put me on the rowing machine, which I promptly sank!

Friday: I hate that son-of-a b**** Bruce more than any human being has ever hated any other human being in the history of the world. Stupid, skinny, anemic little cheerleader wanna-be! If there was a part of my body I could move without unbearable pain, I would beat him with it! Bruce wanted me to work on my triceps. I don't have any triceps!!! And if you don't want dents in the floor don't hand me the %and$#and%and# barbells or anything that weighs more than a sandwich! (which I am sure you learned in the sadist school you attended and graduated magna cum laude!)

The treadmill flung me off and I landed on a health and nutrition teacher. Why couldn't it have been someone softer, like the drama coach of the choir director?

Saturday: Bruce left a message on my answering machine in his grating, shrill voice wondering why I did not show up today. Just hearing him made me want to smash the machine with my planner. However, I lacked the strength to even use the TV remote and ended up catching eleven straight hours of the *and$%^$and weather channel!!!

Sunday: I'm having the Church van pick me up for services today so I can go and thank God that this week is over. I will also pray that next year my husband will choose a gift for me that is fun---- like a root canal or hysterectomy.

A Tale of Tradition

A hard working Chinese rice farmer was supporting his children, wife, and his aging father. He worked long and hard each day, and still, he was barely making enough to feed his children and wife.

One day, he stopped working for the entire day. Instead he built a small cart out of wood he had. The next day he went to his aging father, and insisted that the old man was no longer able to help the family. He was only eating and taking up precious resources. So, he loaded him into the newly built cart, and headed up a nearby mountain.

When he got to the top, he stopped, and aimed the cart facing down the mountain, but before he could roll the cart, his father stopped him saying, "wait, son, I can understand what you are doing, and even why you are doing it, but please save the cart, your son will need it."

A Special Teacher

Years ago a John Hopkins professor gave a group of graduate students this assignment: Go to the slums. Take 200 boys, between the ages of 12 and 16, and investigate their background and environment. Then predict their chances for the future.

The students, after consulting social statistics, talking to the boys, and compiling much data, concluded that 90 percent of the boys would spend some time in jail.

Twenty-five years later another group of graduate students was given the job of testing the prediction. They went back to the same area. Some of the boys - by then men - were still there, a few had died, some had moved away, but they got in touch with 180 of the original 200. They found that only four of the group had ever been sent to jail.

Why was it that these men, who had lived in a breeding place of crime, had such a surprisingly good record? The researchers were continually told: "Well, there was a teacher..."

They pressed further, and found that in 75 percent of the cases it was the same woman. The researchers went to this teacher, now living in a home for retired teachers. How had she exerted this remarkable influence over that group of children? Could she give them any reason why these boys should have remembered her?

"No," she said, "no I really couldn't." And then, thinking back over the years, she said musingly, more to herself than to her questioners: "I loved those boys...."

Listening

When a man whose marriage was in trouble sought his advice, the Master said, "You must learn to listen to your wife."

The man took this advice to heart and returned after a month to say he had learned to listen to every word his wife was saying.

Said the Master with a smile, "Now go home and listen to every word she isn't saying."

Enjoy Life At Every Moment

Once a fisherman was sitting near the seashore, under the shadow of a tree smoking his cigarette. Suddenly a rich businessman passing by approached him and enquired as to why he was sitting under a tree smoking and not working. To this the poor fisherman replied that he had caught enough fishes for the day.

Hearing this the rich man got angry and said: Why don't you catch more fishes instead of sitting in the shadow wasting your time?

The fisherman asked: What would I do by catching more fishes?

Businessman: You could catch more fishes, sell them and earn more money, and buy a bigger boat.

Fisherman: What would I do then?

Businessman: You could go fishing in deep waters and catch even more fishes and earn even more money.

Fisherman: What would I do then?

Businessman: You could buy many boats and employ many people to work for you and earn even more money.

Fisherman: What would I do then?

Businessman: You could become a rich businessman like me.

Fisherman: What would I do then?

Businessman: You could then enjoy your life peacefully.

Fisherman: And what do you think I'm doing right now?

You do not need to wait for tomorrow to be happy and enjoy your life. You don't even need to be more rich or more powerful to enjoy life. LIFE is at this moment, enjoy it fully...

A Lesson From A Mad Hatter

One of the first steps to accomplishing great things in your life is to cease dwelling on the negative things of your past. Carefully assess your present strengths, successes, and achievements. Dwell on those positive events in your life, and quit limiting your potential by constantly thinking about what you have done poorly. Alice and the Mad Hatter in Wonderland had a conversation that illustrates this concept:

Alice: Where I come from, people study what they are not good at in order to be able to do what they are good at.

Mad Hatter: We only go around in circles in Wonderland, but we always end up where we started. Would you mind explaining yourself?

Alice: Well, grown-ups tell us to find out what we did wrong, and never do it again

Mad Hatter: That's odd! It seems to me that in order to find out about something, you have to study it. And when you study it, you should become better at it. Why should you want to become better at something and then never do it again? But please continue.

Alice: Nobody ever tells us to study the right things we do. We're only supposed to learn from the wrong things. But we are permitted to study the right things other people do. And sometimes we're even told to copy them.

Mad Hatter: That's cheating!

Alice: You're quite right, Mr. Hatter. I do live in a topsy-turvy world. It seems like I have to do something wrong first, in order to learn from what not to do. And then, by not doing what I'm not supposed to do, perhaps I'll be right. But I'd rather be right the first time, wouldn't you?

The Dark Candle

A man had a little daughter, a much beloved child. He lived only for her, she was his life. So when she became ill and her illness resisted the efforts of the best obtainable physicians, he did everything to help her, moving heaven and earth to bring about her restoration to health.

His best efforts proved fruitless, however, and the child died. The father was totally devastated. He became a bitter recluse, shutting himself away from his many friends, refusing every activity that might restore his poise and bring him back to his normal self. This was going on for several years.

Then one night he had a dream. He was in heaven and witnessing a grand pageant of all the little child angels. They were marching in an apparently endless line past the Great White Throne. Every white-robed, angelic tot carried a candle. He noticed, however, that one child's candle was not lit. Then he saw that the child with the dark candle was his own little girl. Rushing towards her, while the pageant faltered, he seized her in his arms, caressed her tenderly, and asked, "How is that your candle is the only one not lit?" "Father, they often relight it, but your tears always put it out again," she said.

Just then he awoke from his dream. The lesson was crystal clear, and its effects were immediate. From that day on he was no longer a recluse, but mingled freely and cheerfully with his former friends and associates. No longer would his little darling's candle be extinguished by his useless tears.

A Group of Frogs

As a group of frogs were traveling through the woods, two of them fell into a deep pit. When the other frogs crowded around the pit and saw how deep it was, they told the two frogs that there was no hope left for them.

However, the two frogs decided to ignore what the others were saying and they proceeded to try and jump out of the pit. Despite their efforts, the group of frogs at the top of the pit were still saying that they should just give up. That they would never make it out.

Eventually, one of the frogs took heed to what the others were saying and he gave up, falling down to his death. The other frog continued to jump as hard as he could. Again, the crowd of frogs yelled at him to stop the pain and just die.

He jumped even harder and finally made it out. When he got out, the other frogs said, "Did you not hear us?"

The frog explained to them that he was deaf. He thought

they were encouraging him the entire time.

Moral of the story: People's words can have a big effect on other's lives. Think about what you say before it comes out of your mouth. It might just be the difference between life and death.

Soar Like An Eagle

Did you know that an eagle knows when a storm is approaching long before it breaks?

The eagle will fly to some high spot and wait for the winds to come.

When the storm hits, it sets its wings so that the wind will pick it up and lift it above the storm. While the storm rages below, the eagle is soaring above it.

The eagle does not escape the storm. It simply uses the storm to lift it higher. It rises on the winds that bring the storm.

When the storms of life come upon us, like the eagle, we can rise above them and ride the winds of the storm that bring sickness, tragedy, failure, and disappointment into our lives.

What is your greatest challenge right now? Jot it down. And then let it lift you higher.

Four Burning Candles

In a room there were four candles burning. The ambiance was so soft you could hear them talking.

The first one said, "I am PEACE, however nobody can keep me lit. I believe I will go out."

It's flame rapidly diminishes and goes out completely.

The second one says, "I am FAITH. Most of all I am no longer indispensable, so it does not make any sense that I stay lit any longer."

When it finished talking a breeze softly blew on it putting it out.

Sadly, the third candle spoke in its turn. "I am LOVE. I have not gotten the strength to stay lit. People put me aside and don't understand my importance. They even forget to love those who are nearest to them." And waiting no longer it goes out.

Suddenly a child entered the room and saw three candles not burning. "Why are you not burning you are supposed to stay lit till the end."

Saying this the child began to cry. Then the fourth candle said, "Don't be afraid, while I am still burning we can re-light the other candles, I am HOPE."

With shining eyes, the child took the candle of Hope and lit the other candles.

The flame of Hope should never go out from our life and that each of us can maintain HOPE, FAITH, PEACE and LOVE.

Hope never abandons you. You abandon hope. Consult not your fears but your hopes and your dreams. Think not about your frustrations, but about your unfulfilled potential. Concern yourself not with what you tried and failed in, but with what is still possible for you to do.

Laughter is The Best Medicine

Years ago, Norman Cousins was diagnosed as "terminally ill". He was given six months to live. His chance for recovery was 1 in 500.

He could see the worry, depression and anger in his life contributed to, and perhaps helped cause, his disease. He wondered, "If illness can be caused by negativity, can wellness be created by positivity?"

He decided to make an experiment of himself. Laughter was one of the most positive activities he knew. He rented all the funny movies he could find – Keaton, Chaplin, Fields, the Marx Brothers. He read funny stories. He asked his friends to call him whenever they said, heard or did something funny.

His pain was so great he could not sleep. Laughing for 10 solid minutes, he found, relieved the pain for several hours so he could sleep.

He fully recovered from his illness and lived another 20 happy, healthy and productive years. (His journey is detailed in his book, 'Anatomy of an Illness'.) He credits visualization, the love of his family and friends, and laughter for his recovery.

Some people think laughter is a waste of time. It is a luxury, they say, a frivolity, something to indulge in only every so often.

Nothing could be further from the truth. Laughter is essential to our equilibrium, to our well-being, to our aliveness. If we're not well, laughter helps us get well; if we are well, laughter helps us stay that way.

Since Cousins' ground-breaking subjective work, scientific studies have shown that laughter has a curative effect on the body, the mind and the emotions.

So, if you like laughter, consider it sound medical advice to indulge in it as often as you can. If you don't like laughter, then take your medicine – laugh anyway.

Use whatever makes you laugh – movies, sitcoms, Monty Python, records, books, New Yorker cartoons, jokes, friends.

Give yourself permission to laugh – long and loud and out loud – whenever anything strikes you as funny. The people around you may think you're strange, but sooner or later they'll join in even if they don't know what you're laughing about.

Some diseases may be contagious, but none is as contagious as the cure. . . laughter.

Out of the Box Thinking

In a small Italian town, hundreds of years ago, a small business owner owed a large sum of money to a loan-shark. The loan-shark was an old, unattractive looking guy that just so happened to fancy the business owner's daughter.

He decided to offer the businessman a deal that would completely wipe out the debt he owed him. However, the catch was that he would only wipe out the debt if he could marry the businessman's daughter. Needless to say, this proposal was met with a look of disgust.

The loan-shark said that he would place two pebbles into a bag, one white and one black. The daughter would then have to reach into the bag and pick out a pebble. If it was black, the debt would be wiped, but the loan-shark would then marry her. If it was white, the debt would also be wiped, but the daughter wouldn't have to marry the loan-shark.

Standing on a pebble strewn path in the businessman's garden, the loan-shark bent over and picked up two pebbles. Whilst he was picking them up, the daughter noticed that he'd picked up two black pebbles and placed them both into the bag. He then asked the daughter to reach into the bag and pick one.

The daughter naturally had three choices as to what she could have done:

- Refuse to pick a pebble from the bag.

- Take both pebbles out of the bag and expose the loan-shark for cheating.

- Pick a pebble from the bag fully well knowing it was black and sacrifice herself for her father's freedom.

She drew out a pebble from the bag, and before looking at it 'accidentally' dropped it into the midst of the other pebbles. She then said to the loan-shark;

"Oh, how clumsy of me. Never mind, if you look into the bag for the one that is left, you will be able to tell which pebble I picked."

The pebble left in the bag is obviously black, and seeing as the loan-shark didn't want to be exposed, he had to play along, and clear her father's debt.

Moral of the story: It's always possible to overcome a tough situation through out of the box thinking - do not give in to the "only options" you think you have to pick from.

A Hall Of Mirrors

A long time ago there was a great Shah. He ordered to build a beautiful palace which had many wonderful things in it. Among other curiosities in the palace there was a hall where all the walls, the sealing, the door and even the floor were made of mirrors.

The mirrors were so clear and smooth that visitors didn't understand at first that there was a mirror in front of them so accurately the mirrors would reflect the objects. Moreover, the walls of this hall were made in a way that they created an extraordinary increased echo.

Once, a dog ran into the hall and froze in surprise in the middle of the hall, a whole pack of dogs surrounded it from all sides, from above and below. Just in case, the dog bared his teeth and all the reflections responded to it in the same way.

Frightened, the dog frantically barked and in return the echo imitated the bark and increased it many times. The dog barked even harder and the echo was keeping up. The dog tossed from one side to another, biting the air - his reflections also tossed around snapping their teeth.

In the morning the guards found the miserable dog lifeless and surrounded by a million reflections of lifeless dogs. There was nobody, who would make any harm to the dog. The dog died by fighting with his own reflections.

The world does not bring good or evil on its own. Everything that is happening around us is the reflection of our own thoughts, feelings, wishes and actions. The world is a big mirror.

Strike a good pose! Smile from deep within! Life is beautiful! Stay Positive!

The Important Things In Life

A philosophy professor stood before his class with some items on the table in front of him. When the class began, wordlessly he picked up a very large and empty mayonnaise jar and proceeded to fill it with rocks, about 2 inches in diameter.

He then asked the students if the jar was full. They agreed that it was.

So the professor then picked up a box of pebbles and poured them into the jar. He shook the jar lightly. The pebbles, of course, rolled into the open areas between the rocks.

He then asked the students again if the jar was full. They agreed it was.

The professor picked up a box of sand and poured it into the jar. Of course, the sand filled up the remaining open areas of the jar.

He then asked once more if the jar was full. The students responded with a unanimous "Yes."

"Now," said the professor, "I want you to recognize that this jar represents your life. The rocks are the important things – your family, your spouse, your health, your children – things that if everything else was lost and only they remained, your life would still be full. The pebbles are the other things that matter – like your job, your house, your car. The sand is everything else, the small stuff."

"If you put the sand into the jar first," he continued, "There is no room for the pebbles or the rocks. The same goes for your life. If you spend all your time and energy on the small stuff, you will never have room for the things that are important to you. Pay attention to the things that are critical to your happiness. Spend time with your children, take your spouse out dancing. There will always be time to go to work, clean the house, give a dinner party, or fix the disposal."

"Take care of the rocks first – the things that really matter. Set your priorities right. The rest is just sand."

Hospital Window

Two men, both seriously ill, occupied the same hospital room. One man was allowed to sit up in his bed for an hour each afternoon to help drain the fluid from his lungs. His bed was next to the room's only window. The other man had to spend all his time flat on his back. The men talked for hours on end. They spoke of their wives and families, their homes, their jobs, their involvement in the military service, where they had been on vacation.

Every afternoon when the man in the bed by the window could sit up, he would pass the time by describing to his roommate all the things he could see outside the window.

The man in the other bed began to live for those one hour periods where his world would be broadened and enlivened by all the activity and color of the world outside.

The window overlooked a park with a lovely lake. Ducks and swans played on the water while children sailed their model boats. Young lovers walked arm in arm amidst flowers of every color and a fine view of the city skyline could be seen in the distance.

As the man by the window described all this in exquisite detail, the man on the other side of the room would close his eyes and imagine the picturesque scene.

One warm afternoon the man by the window described a parade passing by. Although the other man couldn't hear the band – he could see it. In his mind's eye as the gentleman by the window portrayed it with descriptive words.

Days and weeks passed.

One morning, the day nurse arrived to bring water for their baths only to find the lifeless body of the man by the window, who had died peacefully in his sleep. She was saddened and called the hospital attendants to take the body away.

As soon as it seemed appropriate, the other man asked if he could be moved next to the window. The nurse was happy to make the switch, and after making sure he was comfortable, she left him alone.

Slowly, painfully, he propped himself up on one elbow to take his first look at the real world outside. He strained to slowly turn and looked out the window only to face a blank wall.

A Gift Of Love!

"Can I see my baby?" the happy new mother asked.

When the bundle was nestled in her arms and she moved the fold of cloth to look upon his tiny face, she gasped. The doctor turned quickly and looked out the tall hospital window. The baby had been born without ears.

Time proved that the baby's hearing was perfect. It was only his appearance that was marred. When he rushed home from school one day and flung himself into his mother's arms, she sighed, knowing that his life was to be a succession of heartbreaks. He blurted out the tragedy. "A boy, a big boy... called me a freak."

He grew up, handsome for his misfortune. A favorite with his fellow students, he might have been class president, but for that. He developed a gift, a talent for literature and music. "But you might mingle with other young people," his mother reproved him, but felt a kindness in her heart.

The boy's father had a session with the family physician. Could nothing be done? "I believe I could graft on a pair of outer ears, if they could be procured," the doctor decided.

Whereupon the search began for a person who would make such a sacrifice for a young man. Two years went by. Then, "You are going to the hospital, Son. Mother and I have someone who will donate the ears you need. But it's a secret," said the father. The operation was a brilliant success, and a new person emerged. His talents blossomed into genius, and school and college became a series of triumphs.

Later he married and entered the diplomatic service. "But I must know!" He urged his father, "Who gave so much for me? I could never do enough for him." "I do not believe you could," said the father, "But the agreement was that you are not to know … not yet." The years kept their profound secret, but the day did come... one of the darkest days that a son must endure. He stood with his father over his mother's casket. Slowly, tenderly, the father stretched forth a hand and raised the thick, reddish-brown hair to reveal that the mother had no outer ears. "Mother said she was glad she never let her hair be cut," he whispered gently, "And nobody ever thought Mother less beautiful, did they?"

Real beauty lies not in the physical appearance, but in the heart. Real treasure lies not in what that can be seen, but what that cannot be seen. Real love lies not in what is done and known, but in what that is done but not known.

Keep Your Dream

I have a friend named Monty Roberts who owns a horse ranch in San Ysidro. He has let me use his house to put on fund-raising events to raise money for youth at risk programs.

The last time I was there he introduced me by saying:

"I want to tell you why I let Jack use my house for this cause. It all goes back to a story about a young man who was the son of an itinerant horse trainer who would go from stable to stable, race track to race track, farm to farm and ranch to ranch, training horses. As a result, the boy's high school career was continually interrupted. When he was a senior, he was asked to write a paper about what he wanted to be and do when he grew up."

"That night he wrote a seven-page paper describing his goal of someday owning a horse ranch. He wrote about his dream in great detail and he even drew a diagram of a 200-acre ranch, showing the location of all the buildings, the stables and the track. Then he drew a detailed floor plan for a 4,000-square-foot house that would sit on a 200-acre dream ranch."

"He put a great deal of his heart into the project and the next day he handed it in to his teacher. Two days later he received his paper back. On the front page was a large red F with a note that read, `See me after class.'"

"The boy with the dream went to see the teacher after class and asked, `Why did I receive an F?'"

"The teacher said, `This is an unrealistic dream for a young boy like you. You have no money. You come from an itinerant family. You have no resources. Owning a horse ranch requires a lot of money. You have to buy the land. You have to pay for the original breeding stock and later you'll have to pay large stud fees. There's no way you could ever do it.' Then the teacher added, `If you will rewrite this paper with a more realistic goal, I will reconsider your grade.'"

"The boy went home and thought about it long and hard. He asked his father what he should do. His father said, "Look, son, you have to make up your own mind on this. However, I think it is a very important decision for you." Finally, after sitting with it for a week, the boy turned in the same paper, making no changes at all.

He stated, "You can keep the F and I'll keep my dream."

Monty then turned to the assembled group and said, "I tell you this story because you are sitting in my 4,000-square-foot house in the middle of my 200-acre horse ranch. I still have that school paper framed over the fireplace."

He added, "The best part of the story is that two summers ago that same schoolteacher brought 30 kids to camp out on my ranch for a week. When the teacher was leaving, she said, 'Look, Monty, I can tell you this now. When I was your teacher, I was something of a dream stealer. During those years I stole a lot of kids' dreams. Fortunately you had enough gumption not to give up on yours.'"

Don't let anyone steal your dreams. Follow your heart, no matter what!

What Goes Around Comes Around

One day a man saw an old lady, stranded on the side of the road, but even in the dim light of day, he could see she needed help. So he pulled up in front of her Mercedes and got out. His Pontiac was still sputtering when he approached her.

Even with the smile on his face, she was worried. No one had stopped to help for the last hour or so. Was he going to hurt her? He didn't look safe; he looked poor and hungry. He could see that she was frightened, standing out there in the cold.

He knew how she felt. It was those chills which only fear can put in you. He said, "I'm here to help you, ma'am. Why don't you wait in the car where it's warm? By the way, my name is Bryan Anderson."

Well, all she had was a flat tire, but for an old lady, that was bad enough. Bryan crawled under the car looking for a place to put the jack, skinning his knuckles a time or two. Soon he was able to change the tire. But he had to get dirty and his hands hurt.

As he was tightening up the lug nuts, she rolled down the window and began to talk to him. She told him that she was from St. Louis and was only just passing through. She couldn't thank him enough for coming to her aid.

Bryan just smiled as he closed her trunk. The lady asked how much she owed him. Any amount would have been all right with her. She already imagined all the awful things that could have happened had he not stopped. Bryan never thought twice about being paid. This was not a job to him. This was helping someone in need, and God knows there were plenty who had given him a hand in the past. He had lived his whole life that way, and it never occurred to him to act any other way.

He told her that if she really wanted to pay him back, the next time she saw someone who needed help, she could give that person the assistance they needed, and Bryan added, "And think of me."

He waited until she started her car and drove off. It had been a cold and depressing day, but he felt good as he headed for home, disappearing into the twilight.

A few miles down the road the lady saw a small cafe. She went in to grab a bite to eat, and take the chill off before she made the last leg of her trip home. It was a dingy looking restaurant. Outside were two old gas pumps. The whole scene was unfamiliar to her.

The waitress came over and brought a clean towel to wipe her wet hair. She had a sweet smile, one that even being on her feet for the whole day couldn't erase. The lady noticed the waitress was nearly eight months pregnant, but she never let the strain and aches change her attitude. The old lady wondered how someone who had so little could be so giving to a stranger. Then she remembered Bryan.

After the lady finished her meal, she paid with a hundred dollar bill. The waitress quickly went to get change for her hundred dollar bill, but the old lady had slipped right out the door. She was gone by the time the waitress came back. The waitress wondered where the lady could be. Then she noticed something written on the napkin.

There were tears in her eyes when she read what the lady wrote: "You don't owe me anything. I have been there too. Somebody once helped me out, the way I'm helping you. If you really want to pay me back, here is what you do, do not let this chain of love end with you." Under the napkin were four more $100 bills.

Well, there were tables to clear, sugar bowls to fill, and people to serve, but the waitress made it through another day. That night when she got home from work and climbed into bed, she was thinking about the money and what the lady had written.

How could the lady have known how much she and her husband needed it? With the baby due next month, it was going to be hard… She knew how worried her husband was, and as he lay sleeping next to her, she gave him a soft kiss and whispered soft and low, "Everything's going to be all right. I love you, Bryan Anderson."

God's Time

A man walked to the top of a hill to talk to God.

The man asked, "God, what's a million years to you?" and God said, "A minute."

Then the man asked, "Well, what's a million dollars to you?" and God said, "A penny."

Then the man asked, "God…..can I have a penny?" and God said, "Sure…..in a minute.

The Cat

A pastor had a kitten that climbed up a tree in his backyard and then was afraid to come down. The pastor coaxed, offered warm milk, etc. The kitty would not come down.

The tree was not sturdy enough to climb, so the pastor decided that if he tied a rope to his car and drove away so that the tree bent down, he could then reach up and get the kitten.

He did all this, checking his progress in the car frequently, then figured if he went just a little bit further, the tree would be bent sufficiently for him to reach the kitten. But as he moved a little further forward, the rope broke.

The tree went "boing!" and the kitten instantly sailed through the air - out of sight.

The pastor felt terrible.

He walked all over the neighborhood asking people if they'd seen a little kitten. No. Nobody had seen a stray kitten. So he prayed, "Lord, I just commit this kitten to your keeping," and went on about his business.

A few days later he was at the grocery store and met one of his church members. He happened to look into her shopping cart and was amazed to see cat food. Now this woman was a cat hater and everyone knew it, so he asked her, "Why are you buying cat food when you hate cats so much?"

She replied, "You won't believe this," and told him how her little girl had been begging her for a cat, but she kept refusing. Then a few days before, the child had begged again, so the Mom finally told her little girl, "Well if God gives you a cat, I'll let you keep it!"

She told the pastor, "I watched my child go out in the yard, get on her knees, and ask God for a cat. And really, Pastor, you won't believe this, but I saw it with my own eyes.

A kitten suddenly came flying out of the blue sky, with its paws outspread, and landed right in front of her."

A Riot in Paris

In the 19th century there was a riot in Paris. A colonel was ordered to disperse it with guns.

After pointing the guns at the crowd he said: "Will all the respectable citizens please leave the square so I can shoot the mob as I'm ordered?"

And the square emptied completely.

Sometimes you just have to ask...

Trust In God

Man : God, can I ask you a question?

God: Sure...

Man: Promise you won't get mad...

God: I promise...

Man : Why did you let so much stuff happen to me today?

God: What do you mean?

Man: Well, I woke up late...

God: Yes

Man: my car took forever to start...

God: Okay...

Man: At lunch they made my sandwich wrong I had to wait...

God: Hummm...

Man: On, the way home, my phone went dead, just as I picked up a call

God: All right..

Man: And on top of it all, when I got home - I just want to soak my feet in my new foot massager and relax. But, it wouldn't work! Nothing went right today! Why did you do that?

God: Let me see, the death Angel was at your bed this morning and I had to send one of my Angels to battle him for your life. I let you sleep through that...

Man: (humbled): Oh!

God: I didn't let your car start because there was a drunk driver on your route that would have hit you if you were on the road.

Man: (Ashamed)

God: The first person who made your sandwich today was sick & I didn't want you to catch what they have, I knew you couldn't afford to miss work.

Man: (Embarrassed): Okay

God: Your phone went dead because the person that was calling you was going to give a false witness about what you said on that call, I didn't even let you talk to them so you would be covered.

Man: (Softly): I see God

God: Oh, and that foot massager, it had a shortage that was going to shut off all the power in your house tonight. I didn't think you wanted to be in the dark.

Man: I'm sorry God.

God: Don't be sorry, just learn to trust me... in all things, the good and the bad.

Man: I will trust you.

God: And don't doubt that my plan for your day is always better than your plan.

Man: I won't God. And let me just tell you God, Thank you for everything today.

God: You're welcome, child. it was just another day being your God and I Love looking after my children...

God Loves You...

The Crochet Tablecloth (True Story)

The brand new pastor and his wife, newly assigned to their first ministry, to reopen a church in urban Brooklyn, arrived in early October excited about their opportunities. When they saw their church, it was very run down and needed much work.

They set a goal to have everything done in time to have their first service on Christmas Eve. They worked hard, repairing pews, plastering walls, painting, etc. and on Dec. 18 were ahead of schedule and just about finished.

On December 19 a terrible tempest - a driving rainstorm hit the area and lasted for two days. On the 21st, the pastor went over to the church. His heart sunk when he saw that the roof had leaked, causing a large area of plaster about 6 feet by 8 feet to fall off the front wall of the sanctuary just behind the pulpit, beginning about head high. The pastor cleaned up the mess on the floor, and not knowing what else to do but postpone the Christmas Eve service, headed home.

On the way he noticed that a local business was having a flea market type sale for charity so he stopped in. One of the items was a beautiful, hand-made, ivory colored, crochet tablecloth with exquisite work, fine colors and a Cross-embroidered right in the center. It was just the right size to cover up the hole in the front wall. He bought it and headed back to the church.

By this time it had started to snow. An older woman running from the opposite direction was trying to catch the bus. She missed it. The pastor invited her to wait in the warm church for the next bus 45 minutes later. She sat in a pew and paid no attention to the pastor while he got a ladder, hangers, etc. to put up the tablecloth as a wall tapestry. The pastor could hardly believe how beautiful it looked and it covered up the entire problem area. Then he noticed the woman walking down the center aisle. Her face was like a sheet.

"Pastor," she asked, "Where did you get that tablecloth?" The pastor explained. The woman asked him to check the lower right corner to see if the initials, EBG were crochet into it there. They were. These were the initials of the woman, and she had made this tablecloth 35 years before, in Austria. The woman could hardly believe it as the pastor told how he had just gotten the tablecloth. The woman explained that before the war she and her husband were well-to-do people in Austria. When the Nazis came, she was forced to leave. Her husband was going to follow her the next week. She was captured, sent to prison and never saw her husband or her home again.

The pastor wanted to give her the tablecloth; but she made the pastor keep it for the church. The pastor insisted on driving her home. That was the least he could do. She lived on the other side of Staten Island and was only in Brooklyn for the day for a housecleaning job.

What a wonderful service they had on Christmas Eve. The church was almost full. The music and the spirit were great. At the end of the service, the pastor and his wife greeted everyone at the door and many said that they would return. One older man, whom the pastor recognized from the neighborhood, continued to sit in one of the pews and stare, and the pastor wondered why he was not leaving.

The man asked him where he got the tablecloth on the front wall because it was identical to one that his wife had made years ago when they lived in Austria before the war and how could there be two tablecloths so much alike? He told the pastor how the Nazis came, how he forced his wife to flee for her safety, and he was supposed to follow her, but he was arrested and put in a concentration camp. He never saw his wife or his home again for all the 35 years in between.

The pastor asked him if he would allow him to take him for a little ride. They drove to Staten Island and to the same house where the pastor had taken the woman three days earlier. He helped the man climb the three flights of stairs to the woman's apartment, knocked on the door and the pastor saw the greatest Christmas reunion he could ever imagine.

(Disseminated by Pastor Rob Reid)

Let Go...

A little child was playing one day with a very valuable vase. He put his hand into it and could not withdraw it. His father too, tried his best, but all in vain. They were thinking of breaking the vase when the father said, "Now, my son, make one more try. Open your hand and hold your fingers out straight as you see me doing, and then pull."

To their astonishment the little fellow said, "O no, father. I couldn't put my fingers out like that, because if I did I would drop my penny."

Smile, if you will - but thousands of us are like that little boy, so busy holding on to the world's worthless penny that we cannot accept liberation. I beg you to drop the trifle in your heart. Surrender! Let go!

Believe The Impossible

Every great achievement was once impossible until someone set a goal to make it a reality.

Lewis Carroll's famous masterpiece Through the Looking Glass contains a story that exemplifies the need to dream the impossible dream. There is a conversation between Alice and the queen, which goes like this:

"I can't believe that!" said Alice.

"Can't you?" the queen said in a pitying tone. "Try again, draw a long breath, and shut your eyes."

Alice laughed. "There's no use trying," she said. "One can't believe impossible things."

"I dare say you haven't had much practice," said the queen. "When I was your age, I always did it for half an hour a day. Why, sometimes I've believed as many as six impossible things before breakfast."

When you dare to dream, many marvels can be accomplished. The trouble is, most people never start dreaming their impossible dream.

How High Can You Jump?

Flea trainers have observed a predictable and strange habit of fleas while training them. Fleas are trained by putting them in a cardboard box with a top on it. The fleas will jump up and hit the top of the cardboard box over and over and over again. As you watch them jump and hit the lid, something very interesting becomes obvious. The fleas continue to jump, but they are no longer jumping high enough to hit the top. Apparently, Excedrin headache 1738 forces them to limit the height of their jump.

When you take off the lid, the fleas continue to jump, but they will not jump out of the box. They won't jump out because they can't jump out. Why? The reason is simple. They have conditioned themselves to jump just so high. Once they have conditioned themselves to jump just so high, that's all they can do!

Many times, people do the same thing. They restrict themselves and never reach their potential. Just like the fleas, they fail to jump higher, thinking they are doing all they can do.

The Culprit of Your Overweight Challenges Has Been Finally Identified

Ever wonder who is to blame for your weight loss suffering? Well, wonder no more. Here's the full story.

And God populated the earth with broccoli and cauliflower and spinach, green and yellow vegetables of all kinds, so Man and Woman would live long and healthy lives.

And Satan created McDonald's. And McDonald's brought forth the 99-cent double-cheeseburger. And Satan said to Man, "You want fries with that?"

And Man said, "Super size them."

And Man gained pounds.

And God created the healthful yogurt, that woman might keep her figure that man found so fair.

And Satan brought forth chocolate.

And woman gained pounds.

And God said, "Try my crispy fresh salad."

And Satan brought forth ice cream.

And woman gained pounds. And God said, "I have sent you heart healthy vegetables and olive oil with which to cook them."

And Satan brought forth chicken-fried steak so big it needed its own platter.

And Man gained pounds and his bad cholesterol went through the roof.

And God brought forth running shoes and Man resolved to lose those extra pounds.

And Satan brought forth cable TV with remote control so Man would not have to toil to change channels between ESPN and ESPN2.

And Man gained pounds.

And God said, "You're running up the score, Devil."

And God brought forth the potato, a vegetable naturally low in fat and brimming with nutrition.

And Satan peeled off the healthful skin and sliced the starchy center into chips and deep-fat fried them. And he created sour cream dip also.

And Man clutched his remote control and ate the potato chips swaddled in cholesterol.

And Satan saw and said, "It is good."

And Man went into cardiac arrest.

And God sighed and created quadruple bypass surgery.

And so, Satan created HMOs.

Camel Skills

A mother and a baby camel were lying around under a tree. Then the baby camel asked, "Why do camels have humps?"

The mother camel considered this and said, "We are desert animals so we have the humps to store water so we can survive with very little water."

The baby camel thought for a moment then said, "Ok…why are our legs long and our feet rounded?"

The mama replied, "They are meant for walking in the desert."

The baby paused. After a beat, the camel asked, "Why are our eyelashes long? Sometimes they get in my way."

The mama responded, "Those long thick eyelashes protect your eyes from the desert sand when it blows in the wind.

The baby thought and thought. Then he said, "I see. So the hump is to store water when we are in the desert, the legs are for walking through the desert and these eye lashes protect my eyes from the desert then why in the Zoo?"

The Lesson: Skills and abilities are only useful if you are in the right place at the right time. Otherwise they go to waste.

Keeper of the Spring

The late Peter Marshall was an eloquent speaker and for several years served as the chaplain of the US Senate. He used to love to tell the story of the "Keeper of the Spring," a quiet forest dweller who lived high above an Austrian village along the eastern slope of the Alps.

The old gentleman had been hired many years earlier by a young town councilman to clear away the debris from the pools of water up in the mountain crevices that fed the lovely spring flowing through their town. With faithful, silent regularity, he patrolled the hills, removed the leaves and branches, and wiped away the silt that would otherwise have choked and contaminated the fresh flow of water. The village soon became a popular attraction for vacationers. Graceful swans floated along the crystal clear spring, the mill wheels of various businesses located near the water turned day and night, farmlands were naturally irrigated, and the view from restaurants was picturesque beyond description.

Years passed. One evening the town council met for its semiannual meeting. As they reviewed the budget, one man's eye caught the salary figure being paid the obscure keeper of the spring. Said the keeper of the purse, "Who is the old man? Why do we keep him on year after year? No one ever sees him. For all we know, the strange ranger of the hills is doing us no good. He isn't necessary any longer." By a unanimous vote, they dispensed with the old man's services.

For several weeks, nothing changed.

By early autumn, the trees began to shed their leaves. Small branches snapped of and fell into the pools, hindering the rushing flow of sparkling water. One afternoon someone noticed a slight yellowish-brown tint in the spring. A few days later, the water was much darker. Within another week, a slimy film covered sections of the water along the banks, and a foul odor was soon detected. The mill wheels moved more slowly, some finally ground to a halt. Swans left, as did the tourists. Clammy fingers of disease and sickness reached deeply into the village.

Quickly, the embarrassed council called a special meeting. Realizing their gross error in judgment, they rehired the old keeper of the spring, and within a few weeks, the veritable river of life began to clear up. The wheels started to turn, and new life returned to the hamlet in the Alps.

Never become discouraged with the seeming smallness of your task, job, or life. Cling fast to the words of Edward Everett Hale: "I am only one, but still I am one. I cannot do everything, but still I can do something; and because I cannot do everything, I will not refuse to do something I can do. " The key to accomplishment is believing that what you can do will make a difference.

Winning The Lottery

There once was a man who wanted to win the lottery. He prayed several times each day, "Lord, let me win the lottery."

He prayed like this day after day after day: "Lord, let me win the lottery." The man kept praying like this for weeks and months and years - everyday the same prayer: "Lord, let me win the lottery."

At one point the man desperately turned his eyes up and said: "O Lord, dear Lord I've been praying to you for years why won't you grant me my wishes?"

To this the heavens parted suddenly and the voice of God came down: "Look, I heard you already. But help me out. At least buy a ticket!"

Moral: Wants and dreams are nothing but wishful thinking unless they are acted upon!

You Can't Achieve Happiness With Selfishness

There is this story of a man who had a dream one night. He dreamed that he died and found himself immediately in a large room. In the room there was a huge banquet table filled with all sorts of delicious foods.

Around the table people were seated who were hungry but the chairs were five feet from the edge of the table and people apparently could not get out of the chairs and their arms were not long enough to reach the food.

In the dream there was a single large spoon, five feet long. Everyone was fighting, quarrelling, pushing each other, trying to grab hold of that spoon. Finally in that awful scene, one strong bully got hold of the spoon.

He reached out, picked up some food, and turned it to feed himself. Only to find out that the spoon was so long that as he held it out he could not touch his mouth. The food fell off. Immediately someone else grabbed the spoon. Again, the person reached far enough to pick up the food, but could not feed himself. In the dream, the man who was observing it all said to his guide, "This is hell to have food and not be able to eat it".

The guide replied, "Where do you think you are? This is hell. But this is not your place. Come with me."

And they went into another room. In this room things were the same as the previous room. People were not able to reach food because of the same reasons. Yet they had a satisfied, pleasant look on their faces. Only then the visitors see the reason why.

Exactly as before, there was only one spoon. It, too, had a handle five feet long. Yet no one was fighting for it. In fact, one man, who held the handle, reached out, picked up the food, and put it into the mouth of someone else, which ate it and was satisfied.

That person then took the spoon by the handle, reached for the food from the table, and put it back to the mouth of the man who had just given him something to eat. And the guide said, "This is heaven".

People who try to achieve happiness with selfishness end up in a hell on earth. If you choose to look for people who have burdens, you might be able to help them. But if you just look for your own happiness, ignoring the needs of those around you, you will lose out altogether.

The Whole World Came Together

The young mother was ready for a few minutes of relaxation after a long and demanding day. However, her young daughter had other plans for her mother's time.

"Read me a story, Mom," the little girl requested. "Give Mommy a few minutes to relax and unwind. Then I'll be happy to read you a story," pleaded the mother.

The little girl was insistent that Mommy read to her now. With a stroke of genius, the mother tore off the back page of the magazine she was reading. It contained a full-page picture of the world. As she tore it into several pieces, Mom asked her daughter to put the picture together and then she would read her a story. Surely this would buy her considerable relaxing moments.

A short time later, the little girl announced the completion of her puzzle project. To her astonishment, the mother found the world picture completely assembled. When she asked her daughter how she managed to do it so quickly, the little girl explained that on the reverse side of the page was the picture of a little girl. "You see, Mommy, when I got the little girl together, the whole world came together."

Each of us has the responsibility to put our world together. It starts by getting ourselves put together. We can become better parents, friends, spouses, employees, and employers. The first step is changing our attitude.

A Flat Tire

One night four college kids stayed out late, partying and having a good time. They paid no mind to the test they had scheduled for the next day and didn't study. In the morning, they hatched a plan to get out of taking their test. They covered themselves with grease and dirt and went to the Dean's office. Once there, they said they had been to a wedding the previous night and on the way back they got a flat tire and had to push the car back to campus.

The Dean listened to their tale of woe he then offered them a retest three days later. They thanked him and accepted his offer.

When the test day arrived, they went to the Dean. The Dean put them all in separate rooms for the test. They were fine with this since they had all studied hard. Then they saw the test. It had 2 questions.

1) Your Name _____ (1 Points)

2) Which tire burst? _____ (99 Points)
Options – (a) Front Left (b) Front Right (c) Back Left (d) Back Right

The lesson: always be responsible and make wise decisions.

How The Poor Live

One day, a father of a very wealthy family took his son on a trip to the country with the firm purpose of showing his son how poor people live. They spent a couple of days and nights on the farm of what would be considered a very poor family. On their return from their trip, the father asked his son, "How was the trip?"

"It was great, Dad."

"Did you see how poor people live?" the father asked.

"Oh yeah," said the son.

"So, tell me, what did you learn from the trip?" asked the father.

The son answered, "I saw that we have one dog and they had four. We have a pool that reaches to the middle of our garden, and they have a creek that has no end. We have imported lanterns in our garden, and they have the stars at night. Our patio reaches to the front yard, and they have the whole horizon. We have a small piece of land to live on, and they have fields that go beyond our sight. We have servants who serve us, but they serve others. We buy our food, but they grow theirs. We have walls around our property to protect us; they have friends to protect them."

The boy's father was speechless.

Then his son added, "Thanks, Dad, for showing me how poor we are."

Your 86,400 Bank Deposit

Imagine you had a bank account that deposited $86,400 each morning. The account carries over no balance from day to day, allows you to keep no cash balance, and every evening cancels whatever part of the amount you had failed to use during the day. What would you do? Draw out every dollar each day!

We all have such a bank. Its name is Time. Every morning, it credits you with 86,400 seconds. Every night it writes off, as lost, whatever time you have failed to use wisely. It carries over no balance from day to day. It allows no overdraft so you can't borrow against yourself or use more time than you have. Each day, the account starts fresh. Each night, it destroys an unused time. If you fail to use the day's deposits, it's your loss and you can't appeal to get it back.

There is never any borrowing time. You can't take a loan out on your time or against someone else's.

The time you have is the time you have and that is that. It is yours to decide how you spend the time. It is never the case of us not having enough time to do things, but the case of whether we want to do them and where they fall in our priorities. The clock is ticking, invest your time wisely in your health, happiness and success.

To know the importance of a YEAR, ask the students who failed the next grade.

To know the importance of a MONTH, ask a mother who gave birth to a premature baby.

To know the importance of a WEEK, ask the editor of a weekly magazine.

To know the importance of an HOUR, ask someone waiting to meet his/her lover.

To know the importance of a MINUTE, ask the person who missed his flight.

To know the importance of a SECOND, ask the person who just avoided an accident.

To know the importance of a MILLISECOND, ask the Olympic silver medalist runner.

The Mouse Trap

A mouse looked through the crack in the wall to see the farmer and his wife open a package. "What food might this contain?" the mouse wondered. He was devastated to discover it was a mousetrap.

Retreating to the farmyard, the mouse proclaimed the warning: "There is a mousetrap in the house! There is a mousetrap in the house!"

The chicken clucked and scratched, raised her head and said, "Mr. Mouse, I can tell this is a grave concern to you, but it is of no consequence to me. I cannot be bothered by it."

The mouse turned to the pig and told him, "There is a mousetrap in the house! There is a mousetrap in the house!" The pig sympathized, but said, "I am so very sorry, Mr. Mouse, but there is nothing I can do about it but pray. Be assured you are in my prayers."

The mouse turned to the cow and said, "There is a mousetrap in the house! There is a mousetrap in the house!" The cow said, "Wow, Mr. Mouse. I'm sorry for you, but it's no skin off my nose."

So, the mouse returned to the house, head down and dejected, to face the farmer's mousetrap alone.

That very night a sound was heard throughout the house – like the sound of a mousetrap catching its prey. The farmer's wife rushed to see what was caught. In the darkness, she did not see it was a venomous snake whose tail the trap had caught. The snake bit the farmer's wife. The farmer rushed her to the hospital and she returned home with a fever.

Everyone knows you treat a fever with fresh chicken soup, so the farmer took his hatchet to the farmyard for the soup's main ingredient. But his wife's sickness continued, so friends and neighbors came to sit with her around the clock. To feed them, the farmer butchered the pig. The farmer's wife did not get well; she died. So many people came for her funeral, the farmer had the cow slaughtered to provide enough meat for all of them.

The mouse looked upon it all from his crack in the wall with great sadness.

So, the next time you hear someone is facing a problem and think it doesn't concern you, remember, when one of us is threatened, we are all at risk. We are all involved in this journey called life. We must keep an eye out for one another and make an extra effort to encourage one another. Each one of us is a vital thread in another person's tapestry.

Grey Hair

A curious child asked his mother: "Mommy, why are some of your hairs turning grey?"

The mother tried to use this occasion to teach her child: "It is because of you, dear. Every bad action of yours will turn one of my hairs grey!"

The child replied innocently: "Now I know why grandmother has only grey hairs on her head."

Wrong Email Address

A couple planed to go on vacation but the wife was on a business trip so husband went to the destination first and his wife would meet him the next day.

When he reached his hotel, he decided to send his wife a quick email.

Unfortunately, when typing her email address, he mistyped a letter and his note was directed instead to an elderly preacher's wife whose husband had passed away only the day before.

When the grieving widow checked her email, she took one look at the monitor, let out a piercing scream, and fell to the floor in a dead faint.

At the sound, her family rushed into the room and saw this note on the screen:

Dearest Wife,

Just got checked in. Everything prepared for your arrival tomorrow.

P.S. Sure is hot down here.

You Will Never Lose Your Value

A popular speaker started off a seminar by holding up a $20 bill. A crowd of 200 had gathered to hear him speak. He asked, "Who would like this $20 bill?"

200 hands went up.

He said, "I am going to give this $20 to one of you but first, let me do this." He crumpled the bill up.

He then asked, "Who still wants it?"

All 200 hands were still raised.

"Well," he replied, "What if I do this?" Then he dropped the bill on the ground and stomped on it with his shoes.

He picked it up, and showed it to the crowd. The bill was all crumpled and dirty.

"Now who still wants it?"

All the hands still went up.

"My friends, I have just showed you a very important lesson. No matter what I did to the money, you still wanted it because it did not decrease in value. It was still worth $20.

Many times in our lives, life crumples us and grinds us into the dirt. We make bad decisions or deal with poor circumstances. We feel worthless. But no matter what has happened or what will happen, you will never lose your value. You are special – Don't ever forget it!

The Obstacles In Our Life

There once was a very wealthy and curious king. This king had a huge stone placed in the middle of a road. Then he hid nearby to see if anyone would try to remove the gigantic rock from the road.

The first people to pass by were some of the king's wealthiest merchants and courtiers. Rather than moving it, they simply walked around it. A few loudly blamed the King for not maintaining the roads. Not one of them tried to move the stone.

Finally, a peasant came along. His arms were full of vegetables. When he got near the stone, rather than simply walking around it as the others had, the peasant put down his load and tried to move the stone to the side of the road. It took a lot of effort but he finally succeeded.

The peasant gathered up his load and was ready to go on his way when he saw a purse lying in the road where the rock had been. The peasant opened the purse. The purse was stuffed full of gold coins and a note from the king. The king's note said the purse's gold was a reward for moving the stone from the road.

This story underlines a principle that many of us never understand: every obstacle presents an opportunity to improve our condition.

The Loser Who Never Gave Up!

When he was a little boy his uncle called him "Sparky", after a comic-strip horse named Spark Plug. School was all but impossible for Sparky.

He failed every subject in the eighth grade. He flunked physics in high school, getting a grade of zero. He also flunked algebra and English. And his record in sports wasn't any better. Though he did manage to make the school's golf team, he promptly lost the only important match of the season. Oh, there was a consolation match; he lost that too.

Throughout his youth, Sparky was awkward socially. It wasn't that the other students disliked him; it's just that no one really cared all that much. In fact, Sparky was astonished if a classmate ever said hello to him outside of school hours. There's no way to tell how he might have done at dating. He never once asked a girl out in high school. He was too afraid of being turned down... or perhaps laughed at. Sparky was a loser. He, his classmates... everyone knew it. So he learned to live with it. He made up his mind early that if things were meant to work out, they would. Otherwise he would content himself with what appeared to be his inevitable mediocrity.

One thing was important to Sparky, however, drawing. He was proud of his artwork. No one else appreciated it. But that didn't seem to matter to him. In his senior year of high school, he submitted some cartoons to the yearbook. The editors rejected the concept. Despite this brush-off, Sparky was convinced of his ability. He even decided to become an artist.

So, after completing high school, Sparky wrote Walt Disney Studios. They asked for samples of his artwork. Despite careful preparation, it too was rejected. One more confirmation that he was a loser.

But Sparky still didn't give up. Instead, he decided to tell his own life's story in cartoons. The main character would be a little boy who symbolized the perpetual loser and chronic underachiever.

You know him well. Because Sparky's cartoon character went on to become a cultural phenomenon of sorts. People readily identified with this "lovable loser." He reminded people of the painful and embarrassing moments from their own past, of their pain and their shared humanity.

The character soon became famous worldwide: "Charlie Brown." And Sparky, the boy whose many failures never kept him from trying, whose work was rejected again and again,... is the highly successful cartoonist Charles Schultz. His cartoon strip, "Peanuts," continues to inspire books, T-shirts and Christmas specials, reminding us, as someone once commented, that life somehow finds a way for all of us, even the losers.

Sparky's story reminds us of a very important principle in life. We all face difficulty and discouragement from time to time. We also have a choice in how we handle it. If we're persistent, if we hold fast to our faith, if we continue to develop our unique talents, who knows what can happen? We may end up with an insight and an ability to inspire that comes only through hardship. In the end, there are no "losers". Some winners just take longer to develop!

A Recipe For Success

Once, there was an older man, who was broke, living in a tiny house and owned a beat up car. He was living off of $99 social security checks. At 65 years of age, he decided things had to change. So he thought about what he had to offer. His friends raved about his chicken recipe. He decided that this was his best shot at making a change.

He left Kentucky and traveled to different states to try to sell his recipe. He told restaurant owners that he had a mouthwatering chicken recipe. He offered the recipe to them for free, just asking for a small percentage on the items sold. Sounds like a good deal, right?

Unfortunately, not to most of the restaurants. He heard NO over 1000 times. Even after all of those rejections, he didn't give up. He believed his chicken recipe was something special. He got rejected 1009 times before he heard his first yes.

With that one success Colonel Hartland Sanders changed the way Americans eat chicken. Kentucky Fried Chicken, popularly known as KFC, was born.

Remember, never give up and always believe in yourself in spite of rejection.

A Dish of Ice Cream

In the days when an ice cream sundae cost much less, a 10 year old boy entered a hotel coffee shop and sat at a table. A waitress put a glass of water in front of him.

"How much is an ice cream sundae?"

"50 cents," replied the waitress.

The little boy pulled his hand out of his pocket and studied a number of coins in it.

"How much is a dish of plain ice cream?" he inquired. Some people were now waiting for a table and the waitress was a bit impatient.

"35 cents," she said brusquely.

The little boy again counted the coins. "I'll have the plain ice cream," he said.

The waitress brought the ice cream, put the bill on the table and walked away. The boy finished the ice cream, paid the cashier and departed.

When the waitress came back, she began wiping down the table and then swallowed hard at what she saw.

There, placed neatly beside the empty dish, were 15 cents – her tip.

A Quiet Scolding

The late John Wanamaker was the king of retail. One day while walking through his store in Philadelphia, he noticed a customer waiting for assistance. No one was paying the least bit of attention to her. Looking around, he saw his salespeople huddled together laughing and talking among themselves. Without a word, he quietly slipped behind the counter and waited on the customer himself. Then he quietly handed the purchase to the salespeople to be wrapped as he went on his way. Later, Wanamaker was quoted as saying, "I learned thirty years ago that it is foolish to scold. I have enough trouble overcoming my own limitations without fretting over the fact that God has not seen fit to distribute evenly the gift of intelligence."

Quick Decisions

A game warden noticed how a particular fellow named Sam consistently caught more fish than anyone else, whereas the other guys would only catch three or four a day. Sam would come in off the lake with a boat full. Stringer after stringer was always packed with freshly caught trout. The warden, curious, asked Sam his secret. The successful fisherman invited the game warden to accompany him and observe. So the next morning the two met at the dock and took off in Sam's boat. When they got to the middle of the lake, Sam stopped the boat, and the warden sat back to see how it was done.

Sam's approach was simple. He took out a stick of dynamite, lit it, and threw it in the air. The explosion rocked the lake with such a force that dead fish immediately began to surface. Sam took out a net and started scooping them up.

Well, you can imagine the reaction of the game warden. When he recovered from the shock of it all, he began yelling at Sam. "You can't do this! I'll put you in jail, buddy! You will be paying every fine there is in the book!" Sam, meanwhile, set his net down and took out another stick of dynamite. He lit it and tossed it in the lap of the game warden with these words, "Are you going to sit there all day complaining, or are you going to fish?"

The poor warden was left with a fast decision to make. He was yanked, in one second, from an observer to a participant. A dynamite of a choice had to be made and be made quickly!

Life is like that. Few days go by without our coming face to face with an uninvited, unanticipated, yet unavoidable decision. Like a crashing snow bank, these decisions tumble upon us without warning. Quick. Immediate. Sudden. No council, no study, no advice. Pow!

A Lesson From A Chef

Once upon a time a daughter complained to her father that her life was miserable and that she didn't know how she was going to make it. She was tired of fighting and struggling all the time. It seemed just as one problem was solved, another one soon followed.

Her father, a chef, took her to the kitchen. He filled three pots with water and placed each on a high fire. Once the three pots began to boil, he placed potatoes in one pot, eggs in the second pot, and ground coffee beans in the third pot.

He then let them sit and boil, without saying a word to his daughter. The daughter, moaned and impatiently waited, wondering what he was doing.

After twenty minutes he turned off the burners. He took the potatoes out of the pot and placed them in a bowl. He pulled the eggs out and placed them in a bowl.

He then ladled the coffee out and placed it in a cup. Turning to her he asked. "Daughter, what do you see?"

"Potatoes, eggs, and coffee," she hastily replied.

"Look closer," he said, "and touch the potatoes." She did and noted that they were soft. He then asked her to take an egg and break it. After pulling off the shell, she observed the hard-boiled egg. Finally, he asked her to sip the coffee. Its rich aroma brought a smile to her face.

"Father, what does this mean?" she asked.

He then explained that the potatoes, the eggs and coffee beans had each faced the same adversity - the boiling water.

However, each one reacted differently.

The potato went in strong, hard, and unrelenting, but in boiling water, it became soft and weak.

The egg was fragile, with the thin outer shell protecting its liquid interior until it was put in the boiling water. Then the inside of the egg became hard.

However, the ground coffee beans were unique. After they were exposed to the boiling water, they changed the water and created something new.

"Which are you," he asked his daughter. "When adversity knocks on your door, how do you respond? Are you a potato, an egg, or a coffee bean? "

In life, things happen around us, things happen to us, but the only thing that truly matters is what happens within us.

Which one are you?

The Elephant Rope

As a man was passing the elephants, he suddenly stopped, confused by the fact that these huge creatures were being held by only a small rope tied to their front leg. No chains, no cages. It was obvious that the elephants could, at anytime, break away from their bonds but for some reason, they did not.

He saw a trainer nearby and asked why these animals just stood there and made no attempt to get away. "Well," the trainer said, "When they are very young and much smaller we use the same size rope to tie them and, at that age, it's enough to hold them. As they grow up, they are conditioned to believe they cannot break away. They believe the rope can still hold them, so they never try to break free."

The man was amazed. These animals could at any time break free from their bonds but because they believed they couldn't, they were stuck right where they were.

Like the elephants, how many of us go through life hanging onto a belief that we cannot do something, simply because we failed at it once before?

Failure is part of learning; we should never give up the struggle in life.

A Tragedy Or a Blessing?

Years ago in Scotland, the Clark family had a dream. Clark and his wife worked and saved, making plans for their nine children and themselves to travel to the United States. It had taken years, but they had finally saved enough money and had gotten passports and reservations for the whole family on a new liner to the United States.

The entire family was filled with anticipation and excitement about their new life. However, seven days before their departure, the youngest son was bitten by a dog. The doctor sewed up the boy but hung a yellow sheet on the Clarks' front door. Because of the possibility of rabies, they were being quarantined for fourteen days.

The family's dreams were dashed. They would not be able to make the trip to America as they had planned. The father, filled with disappointment and anger, stomped to the dock to watch the ship leave - without the Clark family. The father shed tears of disappointment and cursed both his son and God for their misfortune.

Five days later, the tragic news spread throughout Scotland - the mighty Titanic had sunk. The unsinkable ship had sunk, taking hundreds of lives with it. The Clark family was to have been on that ship, but because the son had been bitten by a dog, they were left behind in Scotland.

When Mr. Clark heard the news, he hugged his son and thanked him for saving the family. He thanked God for saving their lives and turning what he had felt was a tragedy into a blessing.

Grind or Shine

Adversity is the grindstone of life. Intended to polish you up, adversity also has the ability to grind you down. The impact and ultimate result depend on what you do with the difficulties that come your way. Consider the phenomenal achievements of people experiencing adversity.

Beethoven composed his greatest works after becoming deaf. Sir Walter Raleigh wrote the History of the World during a thirteen year imprisonment. If Columbus had turned back, no one could have blamed him, considering the constant adversity he endured. Of course, no one would have remembered him either.

Abraham Lincoln achieved greatness by his display of wisdom and character during the devastation of the Civil War. Luther translated the Bible while enduring confinement in the Castle of Wartburg. Under a sentence of death and during twenty years in exile, Dante wrote the Divine Comedy. John Bunyan wrote Pilgrim's Progress in a Bedford jail.

Finally, consider a more recent example. Mary Groda-Lewis endured sixteen years of illiteracy because of unrecognized dyslexia, was committed to a reformatory on two different occasions, and almost died of a stroke while bearing a child. Committed to going to college, she worked at a variety of odd jobs to save money, graduated with her high school equivalency at eighteen, was named Oregon's outstanding Upward Bound student, and finally entered college. Determined to become a doctor, she faced fifteen medical school rejections until Albany Medical College finally accepted her. In 1984, Dr. Mary Groda-Lewis, at thirty-five, graduated with honors to fulfill her dream.

Adversity - the grindstone of life. Will it grind you down or polish you up?

Seeking Happiness

This story is about a beautiful, expensively dressed lady who complained to her psychiatrist that she felt that her whole life was empty, it had no meaning.

So, the lady went to visit a counselor to seek out happiness. The counselor called over the old lady who cleaned the office floors and then said to the rich lady "I am going to ask Mary here to tell you how she found happiness. All I want you to do is listen to her."

So the old lady put down her broom, sat on a chair and told her story: "Well, my husband died of malaria and three months later my only son was killed by a car. I had nobody - I had nothing left. I couldn't sleep, I couldn't eat, I never smiled at anyone, I even thought of taking my own life.

Then one evening a little kitten followed me home from work. Somehow I felt sorry for that kitten. It was cold outside, so I decided to let the kitten in. I got it some milk, and the kitten licked the plate clean. Then it purred and rubbed against my leg and, for the first time in months, I smiled.

Then I stopped to think, if helping a little kitten could make me smile, maybe doing something for people could make me happy.

So the next day I baked some biscuits and took them to a neighbor who was sick in bed.

Every day I tried to do something nice for someone. It made me so happy to see them happy.

Today, I don't know of anybody who sleeps and eats better than I do. I've found happiness, by giving it to others."

When she heard that, the rich lady cried. She had everything that money could buy, but she had lost the things which money cannot buy.

The beauty of life does not depend on how happy you are; but on how happy others can be because of you.

Happiness is not a destination, it's a journey.

Happiness is not tomorrow, it is now.

Happiness is not a dependency, it is a decision.

Happiness is what you are, not what you have!

From Candles to Soap

In 1879, Procter and Gamble's best seller was candles. But the company was in trouble. Thomas Edison had invented the light bulb, and it looked as if candles would become obsolete. Their fears became reality when the market for candles plummeted since they were now sold only for special occasions.

The outlook appeared to be bleak for Procter and Gamble. However, at this time, it seemed that destiny played a dramatic part in pulling the struggling company from the clutches of bankruptcy.

A forgetful employee at a small factory in Cincinnati forgot to turn off his machine when he went to lunch. The result? A frothing mass of lather filled with air bubbles. He almost threw the stuff away but instead decided to make it into soap. The soap floated. Thus, Ivory soap was born and became the mainstay of the Procter and Gamble Company.

Why was soap that floats such a hot item at that time? In Cincinnati, during that period, some people bathed in the Ohio River. Floating soap would never sink and consequently never got lost. So, Ivory soap became a best seller in Ohio and eventually across the country also.

Like Procter and Gamble, never give up when things go wrong or when seemingly insurmountable problems arise. Creativity put to work can change a problem and turn it into a gold mine.

A Ten-Cent Idea

When young F. W. Woolworth was a store clerk, he tried to convince his boss to have a ten-cent sale to reduce inventory. The boss agreed, and the idea was a resounding success. This inspired Woolworth to open his own store and price items at a nickel and a dime. He needed capital for such a venture, so he asked his boss to supply the capital for part interest in the store.

His boss turned him down flat. "The idea is too risky," he told Woolworth. "There are not enough items to sell for five and ten cents." Woolworth went ahead without his boss's backing, and he not only was successful in his first store, but eventually he owned a chain of F. W. Woolworth stores across the nation. Later, his former boss was heard to remark, "As far as I can figure out, every word I used to turn Woolworth down cost me about a million dollars."

Time To Think

Henry Ford hired an efficiency expert to go through his plant. He said, "Find the nonproductive people. Tell me who they are, and I will fire them!"

The expert made the rounds with his clipboard in hand and finally returned to Henry Ford's office with his report. "I've found a problem with one of your administrators," he said. "Every time I walked by, he was sitting with his feet propped up on the desk. The man never does a thing. I definitely think you should consider getting rid of him!" When Henry Ford learned the name of the man the expert was referring to, Ford shook his head and said, "I can't fire him. I pay that man to do nothing but think - and that's what he's doing."

Childish Behavior

A 24 year old boy looking out from the train's window shouted…

"Dad, look the trees are going behind!"

Dad smiled and a young couple sitting nearby looked at the 24 year old's childish behavior with pity, suddenly he again exclaimed…

"Dad, look the clouds are running with us!"

The couple couldn't resist and said to the old man: "Why don't you take your son to a good doctor?" The old man smiled and said... "I did, and we are just coming from the hospital, my son was blind from birth, he just got his eyes today."

Every single person on the planet has a story. Don't judge people before you truly know them. The truth might surprise you.

Wranglers and Stranglers

Years ago there was a group of brilliant young men at the University of Wisconsin, who seemed to have amazing creative literary talent. They were would-be poets, novelists, and essayists. They were extraordinary in their ability to put the English language to its best use. These promising young men met regularly to read and critique each other's work. And critique it they did!

These men were merciless with one another. They dissected the most minute literary expression into a hundred pieces. They were heartless, tough, even mean in their criticism. The sessions became such arenas of literary criticism that the members of this exclusive club called themselves the "Stranglers."

Not to be outdone, the women of literary talent in the university were determined to start a club of their own, one comparable to the Stranglers. They called themselves the "Wranglers." They, too, read their works to one another. But there was one great difference. The criticism was much softer, more positive, more encouraging. Sometimes, there was almost no criticism at all. Every effort, even the most feeble one, was encouraged.

Twenty years later an alumnus of the university was doing an exhaustive study of his classmates' careers when he noticed a vast difference in the literary accomplishments of the Stranglers as opposed to the Wranglers. Of all the bright young men in the Stranglers, not one had made a significant literary accomplishment of any kind. From the Wranglers had come six or more successful writers, some of national renown such as Marjorie Kinnan Rawlings, who wrote 'The Yearling'.

Talent between the two? Probably the same. Level of education? Not much difference. But the Stranglers strangled, while the Wranglers were determined to give each other a lift. The Stranglers promoted an atmosphere of contention and self doubt. The Wranglers highlighted the best, not the worst.

You are Wonderful

The following true story captured our heart. It happened several years ago in the Paris opera house. A famous singer had been contracted to sing, and ticket sales were booming. In fact, the night of the concert found the house packed and every ticket sold.

The feeling of anticipation and excitement was in the air as the house manager took the stage and said, "Ladies and gentlemen, thank you for your enthusiastic support. I am afraid that due to illness, the man whom you've all come to hear will not be performing tonight. However, we have found a suitable substitute we hope will provide you with comparable entertainment." The crowd groaned in disappointment and failed to hear the announcer mention the stand-in's name. The environment turned from excitement to frustration.

The stand-in performer gave the performance everything he had. When he had finished, there was nothing but an uncomfortable silence. No one applauded. Suddenly, from the balcony, a little boy stood up and shouted, "Daddy, I think you are wonderful!" The crowd broke into thunderous applause.

We all need people in our Lives who are willing to stand up once in a while and say, "I think you are wonderful. "

The Miracle Of Love (True Story!)

Like any good mother, when Karen found out that another baby was on the way, she did what she could to help her 3-year-old son, Michael, prepare for a new sibling.

The new baby was going to be a girl, and day after day, night after night, Michael sang to his sister in Mommy's tummy. He was building a bond of love with his little sister before he even met her.

The pregnancy progressed normally for Karen, resident of Morristown, Tennessee, USA.

In time, the labor pains came. Soon it was every five minutes, every three, every minute. But serious complications arose during delivery and Karen found herself in hours of labor.

Finally, after a long struggle, Michael's little sister was born. But she was in very serious condition. With a siren howling in the night, the ambulance rushed the infant to the neonatal intensive care unit at St. Mary's Hospital, Knoxville, Tennessee.

The days inched by. The little girl got worse. The pediatrician had to tell the parents there was very little hope. Be prepared for the worst. Karen and her husband contacted a local cemetery about a burial plot. They had fixed up a special room in their house for their new baby, instead, they found themselves having to plan for a funeral.

Michael, however, kept begging his parents to let him see his sister. "I want to sing to her," he kept saying.

Week two in intensive care looked as if a funeral would come before the week was over. Michael kept nagging about singing to his sister, but kids are never allowed in Intensive Care.

Karen decided to take Michael whether they liked it or not. If he didn't see his sister right then, he may never see her alive. She dressed him in an oversized scrub suit and marched him into ICU. He looked like a walking laundry basket.

The head nurse recognized him as a child and bellowed, "Get that kid out of here now. No children are allowed."

The mother rose up strong in Karen and the usually mild-mannered lady glared steel-eyed right into the head nurse's eyes, her lips a firm line, "He is not leaving until he sings to his sister."

Then Karen towed Michael to his sister's bedside. He gazed at the tiny infant losing the battle to live. After a moment, he began tossing. In the pure-hearted voice of a 3-year-old, Michael sang:

"You are my sunshine, my only sunshine, you make me happy when skies are gray."

Instantly the baby girl seemed to respond. The pulse rate began to calm down and became steady.

"Keep on singing, Michael," encouraged Karen with tears in her eyes.

"You never know, dear, how much I love you, please don't take my sunshine away."

As Michael sang to his sister, the baby's ragged, strained breathing became as smooth as a kitten's purr. "Keep on singing, sweetheart."

"The other night, dear, as I lay sleeping, I dreamed I held you in my arms".

Michael's little sister began to relax as rest, healing rest, seemed to sweep over her. "Keep singing, Michael." Tears had now conquered the face of the bossy head nurse. Karen glowed.

"You are my sunshine, my only sunshine. Please don't take my sunshine away…"

The next day,…the very next day…the little girl was well enough to go home.

The lesson: Never give up on the people you love. Love is so incredibly powerful.

– The Woman's Day Magazine called it, "the miracle of a brother's song".
– The medical staff called it a miracle.
– Karen called it a miracle of love.

This is a true story, happened in 1992 in Tennessee, USA. The baby girl's name is Marlee.

* * * *